Journey around the Bible

An introduction for beginners

Richard Tarr

Copyright © 2023 Richard Tarr

All rights reserved.

ISBN: 9798857764657

DEDICATION

To those, too many to mention, who helped me with my own journey.

CONTENTS

Acknowledgments

1 Preface

2 How to use this book

3 Journey around the Bible

ACKNOWLEDGMENTS

For Rachel, my wife and our children Georgia and Samuel.

Preface

Years before I became a Christian and troubled by a nagging sense that I should find out once and for all whether this God was real or not, I embarked on a systematic read of the Bible. I began at Genesis but I called a halt early, at the end of the Old Testament, a respectable compromise point I thought. The reason I abandoned it was that it was just doing nothing for me. From a historical point of view I didn't know if what I was reading was true. As for learning other 'truths' like what was the meaning of life, I found the Bible just bounced off me, making no such impact. Following the abandonment of the Bible I also gave up my search for God. Later in life and against my will, I was confronted with the same questions, and having been led by another route, I made the leap of faith and committed myself to God. It was then that when reading the Bible it came alive for me. Its 'truths' I mentioned before, instead of bouncing off, now penetrated me. By this I mean that beautifully and coherently the Bible revealed who I was and also who God was. The Old Testament, the story of a nations struggle to live rightly, with purpose, meaning and with God, was the story of my life. The New Testament, the story of how God came to rescue His people from their failure, was the story of what God had done for me. This was an incredibly exciting discovery. It was then that I realised that the Bible was a spiritual book and that by getting to know the Bible I was getting to know God.

This is my attempt to explain the integrity and authority of the Bible. To give readers a taste of why the Bible can be relied upon as a compilation of historical documents and to show that it is more than a collection of moral messages, legends or children's stories. It is not comprehensive and will probably raise more questions than it answers, but I hope it will start a reader's investigation into this much owned, but little read book. That way you won't have to take my word for what I've said about *the* Word.

How to use this book

This is a six week plan to introduce people to the Bible. It selects 42 chapters from the Bible that try to encapsulate the overall message of the work of God's salvation for the world and provides a commentary to help people understand the world's most popular book. It is aimed at adults either new to the faith or those investigating it.

To accompany this guide you will need a Bible. It doesn't matter too much which translation you use. I don't personally have strong feelings as to what is the best one to use. At home I use the English Standard Version (ESV). The church we attend uses the New International Version (NIV). It might be worthwhile just making a note here about different translations of the Bible because a question new believers often have is why are there so many versions?

The first thing to say is that good translations are done by committees of scholars educated in the ancient languages of the Bible. They translate in teams so as to prevent an individual's bias from affecting the accuracy of the translations. This is because, as people steeped in the word of God, their desire is for it to be produced truthful version of the original.

That still begs the question, why are they not all the same? The short answer is that biblical languages often don't have a like-for-like equivalent found in modern languages. That means a translator today has to choose a word or phrase they think best expresses what the original writer intended. That way, although the words may differ, the meaning remains the same. Also, Bibles are translated for different audiences. For example, one aimed at the scholar might be less concerned with the flow and style because that is not what the reader is interested in. If you are not reading for academic purposes (ESV), an easy-to-read style might be your preference (NIV). Some are translated for younger readers (GNB), some like older forms that date back to the time of Shakespeare (KJV), because they love the beauty of the verse.

You may already have a preference. Those in brackets above are just examples, but any one of them would work. A quick google search can give you some other ideas. All I would say is look for a translation not an interpretation. That way you won't go far wrong in reading a version that tries to stay as close as possible to the original meaning.

Each day of the plan suggests a chapter to read and provides a section on 'knowing the Bible' and 'knowing God'. The former is designed to place the passage for the day in historical and theological context. The latter section is to provide a thought to read on what the passage might mean in the reader's own spiritual journey. The readings could be approached in the following ways:

1. Each day read 'Know the Bible' first, which will help provide a context for the chapter you are about to read. Then, read the relevant Bible chapter followed by 'Knowing God'. This is how the pages are set out but it is not essential to use it as such.
2. Each day read the relevant Bible chapter followed by the two "know" sections.
3. Read 'Knowing the Bible' with the relevant chapter in the morning. In the evening read the chapter again followed by 'Knowing God'. The benefit of this is that by reading the biblical chapter twice in one day, your familiarity with the text will grow stronger. You will also have possibly had time to reflect on what you had read in the morning during the course of your

day, which will aid you in your understanding of the 'Knowing God' section in the evening.
4. Approach the book as an 84 day study, dividing each study into the two "know" sections, one to be looked at each day.

Day 1

Knowing the Bible

There are two parts of the Bible, the Old and New Testament. Altogether it has 66 books, 39 in the Old and 27 in the New. The object of the Christian faith, Jesus Christ, appears at the beginning of the New Testament. This is about three quarters of the way through the Bible and in the gospels (meaning 'good news') of Matthew, Mark, Luke and John. Luke is the most detailed in the account of Jesus' early life and curiously tells us of people we have not heard from before and never hear of again: Simeon, Anna and Phanuel.

Luke, a doctor, possibly writing about 30-40 years after the life of Christ, bases his narrative on eyewitness accounts of those who knew Jesus. Although the names he mentions remain obscure to modern readers, their appearance gives authority to the claim that Luke was party to intimate knowledge of Jesus' life and credence to the belief that this is a historical document. Had Luke been errant in his work, there would have been witnesses and relatives who would have challenged his version of events. As you will see in his sequel book, 'Acts of the Apostles', Luke proves to be a conscientious and credible historian.

Read the Gospel of Luke, chapter 2: Jesus' birth and childhood.

Knowing God

There is no doubt that Luke, those he named as witnesses and his intended readers, would have believed in the fantastic events describing the birth of Jesus. This book too will treat the Bible as the true Word of God, in part as the direct words given by God, partly as written by men under the guidance and inspiration of God's Holy Spirit. At the start of our journey it would be useful to consider how it is that Christians approach the Bible and its more miraculous stories. Non-Christians may argue that such impossible events cannot take place. These stories do not fit in with the scientific mindset of today. Therefore, if people cannot believe these things happened then they will not believe in this God. As a result people come to the conclusion that God does not exist. However, a Christian response would be thus: if we assume for now that it is possible for a great and divine mind to exist that did create life the universe and everything, how hard can it be for this same God to perform other smaller, unique acts like the ones described in Luke's Gospel so far? If the Bible is approached with an openness to the possibilities of a God that does exist, then it may be that He will speak to you through the rest of your study.

Day 2

Knowing the Bible

Mark's Gospel is one of relentless action, written as if by someone present like a reporter making notes as the breathless chain of events unfolds. Mark, it is revealed in the New Testament and in some writings in the early church, was a close associate of Peter, who we will see became Jesus' right hand man. It is from this friendship that it is believed Mark got his information about the life of Christ. Mark's Gospel is the earliest and provided Matthew and Luke with information they used in their own Gospels. However, it has been suggested that Mark made an anonymous cameo appearance in the Gospel which places him even closer to the action – check out Mark chapter 14, verse 51 for the strange case of the naked youth! Some believe that this is Mark's signature on his work.

Read the Gospel of Mark, chapter 1: the start of His ministry.

Knowing God

'Submission' is a bit of a dirty word – it smacks of giving up, of weakness. If you come to this study having already made a commitment to follow Christ you will at some level have already submitted. Rather than this being a humiliating experience, your submission will be one that has led to a sense of peace, hope and excitement. If you come to this study without any Christian belief, the very fact that you are taking the time to do this suggests that you are at least curious to find out about a book that talks about a way of living that is different to the dominant culture of today. In an age of self-gratification, the idea of submission may not sound attractive but if we are to question whether society's values are really the ones we want and would consider alternative ones, then we may have to be prepared to turn certain ideas on their head. Accepting submission is one of these. Look at the first chapter of Mark and notice the importance of it. Jesus, God's own son decides that as His act of submission to His Father's will, He will be publicly baptised. The disciples in turn do the same thing, submitting themselves to Jesus (God in flesh). As a result of this a work of great power is unleashed with powerful preaching, healing and even exorcisms. It is God that is capable of these great things and by submitting your life to Him He is free to do these things in you.

Day 3

Knowing the Bible

In the last reading in Mark's Gospel we saw the urgency of Christ's ministry (work). Today we have in Matthew chapter nine one urgent day in Jesus' life. Matthew's is the second Gospel to be written (about 70-80AD) and from its concerns and style it appears to be aimed at Jewish converts to Christianity. Remember, Jesus was a Jew and the vast majority of early believers in Jesus were Jewish. In fact, the word 'Christian' (meaning "to be Christ-like") does not exist until after Jesus' death. The earliest followers of Jesus would have still regarded themselves as Jewish, but followers of the true message of God given to the Jews. Rather than seeing the Jews that did not recognise Jesus as being of a different religion, these believers saw their fellow Jews as missing out on the truth by failing to realise Jesus was sent by God. It was years before Christianity came to be a separate religion rather than as another branch of Judaism.

In this chapter notice the economy of the words used to describe the most incredible of things – you need to ponder each event in itself to appreciate the furore each scene would have created. The seeds of the conflict and divide that Jesus brought to Israel are sown here. Already He is either loved or hated, followed or condemned. Jesus Christ, weak and mild? If that was your perception prior to this study think again and stay with this study – your perception is likely to change.

Read the Gospel of Matthew, chapter 9: a day in His life.

Knowing God

In another part of the Bible truth is likened to a sword. A sword divides what it strikes. What a sword divides cannot be put back together. Jesus cuts through Israelite society like the proverbial knife through butter. It was soon clear that such was His power in preaching and healing that the old order of society which was dominated by the religious authorities would change forever, and it did. We live in a world where we are told that truth is what you make it, what is true for you, may not be true for someone else but that doesn't matter because someone else can have their own truth. But by definition truth cannot be things that contradict each other. For example if someone is brought before a court on trial of theft, they are either guilty or not - they cannot be both guilty and innocent. I once saw a debate between a Christian and a non-believer on TV about the existence of God. The latter in reply to the argument put in favour of the existence of God said "that is great, that is true, but for you. What is true for me is..." and they proceeded to explain. But this is utter rubbish. Either He is truth and therefore He is whom we have to centre our lives upon or Christianity is false and we have no choice but to dismiss Him — this is the stark choice Jesus leaves the witnesses in this chapter to make. Today, having considered the evidence before us in the Bible, we have to do the same thing.

Day 4

Knowing the Bible

It is impossible to do justice to such teaching in one day's study but here we have a collection of Jesus' sayings which were delivered in His message known as the Sermon on the Plain. This title might sound slightly familiar – in Matthew's Gospel we have the Sermon on the Mount which contains a lot of the same teaching. You will find between the Gospels that a lot of the teaching is the same – you'd be worried about whether they were genuinely Christ's if they weren't. It is also reasonable to assume that in the absence of recording facilities, Jesus did repeat His messages at times. Also, in the ancient world, taking the work of one writer and using their material in your own was seen as a compliment to the credibility and authority of the original work. That the same teaching appears in different contexts shouldn't trouble us. Remember that the Gospels are not history books, they are a unique type of book that takes real events and instead of presenting them in order of their occurrence, the authors have skilfully woven an account that best teaches the particular audience they were writing for.

Read the Gospel of Luke, chapter 6: a summary of His teaching.

Knowing God

A not uncommon response to the more difficult teaching of Christ is to say "no-one can be like that so there is no point trying". This is understandable when you look at the list of things we should be: loving towards our enemies; giving away our clothes; lending money with no expectation of getting it back; avoiding judging others; giving to everyone who asks; not demanding back what has been stolen from us and forgiving those who hurt us. What makes this all the more difficult is when we have a proper understanding of the word 'blessed'. To be blessed means to have an other-worldly or heavenly peace and joy regardless of our circumstances. You will be happy in all situations you are in including the bad ones. Impossible to us? Yes. This is where the submission to Christ that was mentioned before becomes important, because whilst we remain in control of our lives we cannot change ourselves to become these people. It will be the power of Him in us that will make the standards Jesus set possible to reach. Think of it this way: you have learnt to drive and have bought your first car. You have an important journey to make and you get into your vehicle. You put the key in the ignition but do not turn it. You want to make this trip on your own but because you are not using the power given to you to complete your journey, you will be frustrated that you are not getting anywhere. In order to complete your journey you need to ignite the power necessary to do it. Christ is the unseen engine that is the power to take you to places you'd never imagine you would get. If it is not turned on you cannot expect to get to these places. How you can turn on God's power to work in your life so that you can be the character that He describes in Luke, will be the subject of a later study when we look at the Holy Spirit. For now be content to look on this picture Jesus has painted of what you could become with the awe of someone who is admiring a recently acquired work of art hanging on their wall.

Day 5.

Knowing the Bible

The title that Jesus is given here by Peter, "Christ", is a Greek word. It means "anointed one" and to believers, chosen by God. The Hebrew equivalent is "Messiah". In ancient Israel oil was poured onto the head of those appointed as King as a sign that they had been sent with God's power and authority.

Jesus calls Himself the "Son of Man" and there are several interpretations of its meaning. Firstly, that it was just a common way of referring to yourself in the way a well spoken person today might use the word "one" in talking about oneself. For example "what is one to do?" Secondly, that it is a term to highlight Jesus' humanity and His willingness to come and serve. Thirdly, it is the same title used in the Old Testament book of Daniel to describe the Messiah. By calling Jesus the Son of Man, He is being identified as the Messiah, the anointed one who will save His people.

Read the Gospel of Luke, chapter 9: "who do you say that I am?"

Knowing God

Never did Jesus ever use the word "Christian" to describe a follower. Jesus used a word that believers still use today: "disciples". This means "student, follower". Right at the beginning and at the end of this chapter we see the cost of discipleship in terms of commitment. For such devotion His followers had to be more than curious about Him, more even than impressed by Him. They would have had to have been convinced by Him. If we accept what we have read so far as true, then their belief in Him is hardly surprising. In fact it is more surprising that so many opposed and were offended by Him. What then, so convinced His disciples? After all they were grounded men, experienced in life, workers in tough, male-dominated trades, unlikely to fall for some lunatic and His soft-headed ideas about God. What red-blooded man will admit love and devotion to one he is not related to? Well, often truth is stranger than fiction and it has been said that some things that appear outrageous are often too amazing to be credibly made up. If the gospel writers had wanted to deceive people they could have made up something a bit more believable. It is seen in this chapter that some thought Jesus a prophet – an admirable position to hold, but He and Peter knew that Jesus was more than that. CS Lewis famously gave us three options when it came to making our minds up about Jesus: he was either a liar, lunatic or Lord. Was He a liar? Already we have seen how He divided people and taught them things about Himself, that if he knew were not true, could only mean that He was the opposite of kind. For example, He taught more about hell than heaven – hardly a kind thing to warn us about if He didn't have the authority to talk about it. However, a deluded liar is quickly found out and is unable to sustain their position for long. There is no whiff of scandal about Jesus' integrity and honesty throughout His life. So He wasn't a liar. We are then left with the other two options. The second, was that He was a lunatic. Read His claims in verse 21-23 and 26-27 and this seems a fair description. However, can the label "lunatic" be given to the man when we consider His insightful teachings and the lucidity with which He brings them? His teachings that have stood the test of time and been described by some, such as Gandhi, as the high point of human ethical teaching. Jesus was no lunatic. The final option is the most outrageous, but also strangely the most believable. He is who He says He is. Jesus is Lord.

Day 6

Knowing the Bible

Parables have been described as 'earthly stories with a heavenly meaning'. Jesus used parables a lot to teach listeners moral and spiritual truths. Often, He is explaining what the world would be like if God's rule was allowed on earth. That is not to say that God is incapable of enforcing His rule upon us but that in His love and mercy He chooses not to force us into following Him. Christians pray that His "kingdom come" in the 'Lord's Prayer'. In other words, for the Kingdom of God to be found on earth.

Parables were a common way for people in Jesus' culture to teach truths and He may even have adapted some existing ones for His own purpose. In an age with few ways of recording what has been said, religious teaching had to be memorable. Jesus told parables that resonated with the lives of His listeners and were therefore often set in agricultural landscapes. However, we would be mistaken if we were to think of these tales as simplistic and easy to understand. Jesus often engaged His enemies in His stories before hitting them with a punch line that hurt. Also, some of the parables are clearly not easy to understand because, as He says in another passage, it is Jesus' desire that we seek God. A believer should never be satisfied with their knowledge of God and should always look to know Him more. Discovering the meaning of the parables is one way of doing this.

Read the Gospel of Luke, chapter 15: lost and found parables.

Knowing God

All three parables tell us of something or someone that has been lost. There are a variety of meanings that can be drawn out from these but common in all of them is the value that God places on everyone.

Earlier in this study we talked about how God's values can be very different from the world's. On day two the example given was the idea of submission. In the same way, these parables teach us of a God who sees things differently. In our throw-away world in which it is said that we know the price of everything and the value of nothing, it is good to know of a God that places a value on everyone. In these parables God is the one who is looking for us and the sheep, coin and son represent those who are not with Him. The parables use the physical environment to explain a spiritual place. In other words, God wants us in His Kingdom, but this isn't a location as in the story, but a place close to Him spiritually, emotionally and mentally. He wants us in close contact. God is not content with having as many people as possible in His Kingdom, but everyone. This is not for His sake – He doesn't need us. It is for our sake because being in God's Kingdom, whether it is in heaven when we die or now on earth, is the best place to be.

In the parable of the Lost Son we see Jesus land a powerful punch line. In the story He describes the suffering of the son who wasted His inheritance in sinful living. Jesus' listeners, who would have resented the way He helped sinners, would at last have cause to celebrate – finally Jesus is condemning those who do wrong. Then at the end Jesus hits the self-righteous listeners – the Father welcomes back the lost son and criticises the judgemental attitude of the older son. Can you imagine the look on the listeners faces?

Day 7

Knowing the Bible

Some of Jesus' parables are more complex than the others and the context needs to be understood before the meaning can be explained.

In the parable of the ten virgins we have an insight into the wedding traditions of the day. They were often several days long with the reception before the ceremony. Anyone who has had to wait for a bride to turn up late to her wedding should have some sympathy with these people – it was traditional for the bridegroom to turn up after two or three days either to meet or arrive with his bride. In the Bible the bridegroom was a symbol of Christ and this parable reminds us of the Christian belief that at the end of time Jesus will return. The next parable again talks of the master's return. It is interesting that the word used for a currency, 'talent', has been adopted into our language with a slightly different meaning. This parable has been used to encourage us to use our God-given talents (abilities) to help His Kingdom grow. Lastly, the story of the 'Sheep and the Goats' tells us of how God will judge us at the end. It is interesting to note that because of the types of breed in the region of Palestine where this story is based, it is very hard to tell the difference between sheep and goats just by looking at them. This parable reminds us that outward appearance tells us little about the nature of a person but that we have a God who knows everything.

Read the Gospel of Matthew, chapter 25: parables of faithfulness.

Knowing God

You maybe by now finding out that the God of the Bible is not the God you thought He was – He is full of surprises. After reading previously of a God in Luke's Gospel who seeks after us, here we read of a God who wants us to do our bit. When you live in God's Kingdom it means you accept Him as your King. The Kingdom is not something you live in, it is something that lives in you. He is not a despotic ruler. Everything you need to live a life for His Kingdom is provided for you. In the Parable of the Ten Virgins what is provided is oil. This has been interpreted as the Holy Spirit. For a Christian this is what God equips us with, His very Spirit, so that we can carry out His work. Christians are not expected to carry out the King's work without the King's power. With His power comes the gifts of the Spirit listed elsewhere in the Bible: love, joy, peace, patience, kindness, goodness, faithfulness, gentleness and self-control. Not only that but these gifts will be of a kind that you were not born with or will ever learn to have by just using your own abilities. Nonetheless, if God has given us His Holy Spirit to dwell in us, these parables remind us that it is not enough to sit on this possession. When we accept Him as our King, His Holy Spirit is not ours to horde. We are required to help expand His Kingdom, not in land but in believers.

Day 8

Knowing the Bible

Here we come across the Gospel of John for the first time. He was one of Jesus' inner circle of disciples that also included Peter and Jesus' brother James. It is very different to the other three Gospels, Matthew, Mark and Luke. These three are known as the 'Synoptic Gospels'. The word synoptic comes from another word meaning 'seen together'. In other words, it seems that those three used the same sources for their work, such are their similarities. John, though, has some unique information about the life of Christ and he arranges the material in a very different way to the others. Perhaps because John used different material, some questioned whether his gospel was historically reliable. However, this perception that John is not concerned with history is not due to a lack of historical detail on John's part, far from it. It is just that for a long time, the immensely rich theology and Christology (study in who Jesus is), overshadowed the huge amount of local knowledge John exhibits of the individuals and places that he included in his gospel. An example of this is the discovery in the twentieth century of the pool of Bethesda near the old Temple. There is no mention of it anywhere else in the Bible and for years the story John tells of the man healed there was regarded as in part fiction. However, the pool's discovery lent weight to the idea that the Gospel of John was a work to be taken as a serious historical document.

On a completely different note, observe the theme of Christ as the bridegroom occurring again.

Read the Gospel of John, chapter 3: sincerity is not enough.

Knowing God

John 3:16 has been described as the "gospel in a nutshell". Not John's Gospel, but the whole of the 'good news' about Jesus Christ. This is the phrase that can be seen on banners at gatherings of large numbers of people such as sporting events and national celebrations. It is a reminder to us that even though we honour or adore sports men and women or national figures, there is a King who is higher and who ultimately puts these things into perspective. In this chapter John gives us a glimpse of the well-known first century figure Nicodemus, who, though an important leader in his day, was starting to question his own perspective. He sincerely wanted to know how to attain the Kingdom of God and it is here we hear the phrase "born again" first coined. Without intending to simplify the teaching on what it is to be born again, basically it means that although we are physically alive, we are all spiritually dead until we are born again. We are all born with a spiritual side, but like the car in our earlier study, our Spirit needs igniting. This birth is not physical, but spiritual and will lead to fullness of life. This is not only the promise of fullness in life now, but of a place in heaven when we die. So far our study has highlighted the different life God might offer us if we submit to Him and are prepared to have our lives turned around or maybe even turned upside down. We know that we are capable of some small change in our lives but that in our own strength we cannot tackle the root cause of our struggles. Jesus teaches that if we want what the Kingdom of God offers then we must be born again.

Day 9

Knowing the Bible

Here, not for the first time, Jesus refers to Himself as one person of the Trinity. Although He doesn't use the word, He talks of Himself as being equal to God. His use of the phrase "I am" for many Jews was a blasphemous one because that was a term that only God used to describe Himself. It is true that Jesus also talks about Himself as under the authority of the Father, suggesting He is some way inferior to the Father. This has been used to suggest that Jesus contradicts Himself. If that were the case, it rather begs the questions, why didn't the Bible writers and translators over the years edit out the contradiction? Or how did Christianity survive if there is such blatant contradiction in its core, essential teaching? Recently I was driving between two rural destinations and just outside the first at the side of the road was an ancient road sign. It was about two foot tall and made of stone. It had painted onto it the distance of the next village. For some reason I decided to test this by making a mental note on my speedometer. To my surprise that ancient road sign was correct – I arrived at the next village after the exact amount of miles it said I would. Why should I have been surprised? Just because the sign was old I had assumed that it must be faulty, that the primitive persons who put up that sign were bound to be mistaken. But people in the past, though lacking the technology we have today were still as intelligent as we are and we shouldn't patronise them by presuming that they were more naïve than us. It is the same with the Bible. At times there are parts that appear to say things contrary to what other parts say. But that is to discredit the utter devotion and scrupulous work that goes into translating the Bible and faithfully passing it on. In other words, if there was such a contradiction, why do we not think the writers would see this? Perhaps it is testimony to the truth of what was said that even when the story is difficult, the writer doesn't remove it but still includes it.

An in depth explanation of the Trinity is not within the scope of this book but perhaps the following analogy will help for now: Christians believe that the Trinity consists of Father, Son and Holy Spirit, all equal, all performing different roles, working together for us and united in the 'Godhead'. Christians believe in one God and the mystery of the Trinity is how one God can be three persons. One way the Trinity has been explained is thus: if you take one lit candle and use it to light two others, each will work separately from the other, all equal in size and it is impossible to tell which one came first. Yet they have all come from the same flame.

Read the Gospel of John, chapter 14: His final instructions.

Knowing God

Here Jesus lays down who He is and what is to come for His disciples. People often say that they'll believe in God when they see Him with their own eyes. Well, here are men confronted with that and still failing to understand. You might say that if the closest people to Him didn't recognise Him as from God, then He probably wasn't. Alternatively, it could be argued that the disciples were just like us - it doesn't matter how God makes Himself known to us, we will still fail to grasp Him, either because we have our own ideas about what He should be like or we simply don't want to hear it. Here Jesus is saying "I am not a symbol of who God is, I am Him. My teaching and work are not just guides to follow, my teaching and work needs to be living in you. Do not believe in a way of doing things, believe in me and the Holy Spirit will show you the way to do things. Christianity is a relationship with me – come to me".

Day 10

Knowing the Bible

There are two main ways of getting in touch with God. One is reading the Bible, the other is through prayer. The relationship described yesterday is like any – it keeps going when the lines of communication are kept open. We have an image of Jesus, who knows what it is like to be human, acting as our advocate before the Father. The

Bible teaches us that God can be influenced by our prayers and answer our hearts desire. Yesterday Jesus talked about giving whatever we ask for in His name. Be careful, we cannot just utter His name after a prayer and expect to get our own way. Don't forget that God is in possession of the maker's manual – He knows what is best for us and we have to admit that often what we think is for our own good is actually the last thing we need. Try to see prayer not as an attempt to manipulate God into giving you what you want, but as a line of communication that reveals to you what God wants for you. When you have the conviction that you know what He wants for you, you will want the same thing. Then when it comes true, your prayer will have been answered.

Notice the difference with another way of communicating – by sending post. When I stick a stamp on an envelope I am stating that I am sending this in the Monarch's name, as it is his or her head that is on it. This should be the guarantee that my communication will arrive. I do not have a personal relationship with the Monarch. With Christ it is not enough that I stamp His name on the communication, I must have a relationship with Him to expect the communication to elicit the response I want.

Read the Gospel of John, chapter 17: His prayer for His followers.

Knowing God

If we are going to compare prayer to other forms of communication, in terms of response times, it may have more in common with emails – you may get an instant reply or it could be a long while before you hear back.

Part of Jesus' prayer is that the disciples will be 'sanctified'. We can be sure that if we are a modern disciple, then Jesus repeats this prayer on our behalf today. The word sanctified comes from the same as 'sanctity' and 'sacred'. In plain English it means to be "set apart". In other words, despite Christians needing to be real and living in the world, they are expected to stand out from the crowd in the way they conduct themselves. There is not enough room here to list how believer's lives should change. But remember, as we read earlier, Christians are equipped with the Holy Spirit to do this. From the drug addict who experiences a painless 'cold turkey', to the adulterer who struggles for years to overcome their problem with lust, the Holy Spirit can effect that change. Most believer's stories are a combination of both of these – some change is painless, some painful, but it all works for good. That is what 'sanctification' is: God sets us apart and by the power and healing of the Holy Spirit sets to work on us. Sanctification is a process of life regeneration. We will not be perfected in this life but God is working in us to make us more 'Christ-like', which is what the word 'Christian' originally meant.

Day 11.

Knowing the Bible

Caiaphus (pronounced: Kiafus), the High Priest, appears twice in this passage and until the twentieth century this was all that history taught us of him. However, archaeologists have recently found the home of a wealthy first century person by that name within the old city wall of Jerusalem.

In all of the four gospels we have a large increase in the amount of detail around the events of the coming days. This demonstrates the paramount importance of this stage of Christ's life, as does the close resemblance of each account. Peter and his friends would have been aware that the Gospels were being compiled. Peter had also been chosen by Jesus to lead the church. Despite that the accounts of Peter's less than glorious behaviour are not removed from the gospels. Testament again to the integrity of the witnesses who brought us the Bible.

Jesus, His followers and a larger proportion of the nation of Israel were in Jerusalem at this time. This was the time of the Passover festival which originates from the event approximately 1400 years before Christ when Moses led the Hebrews (Jews) out of slavery in Egypt. This escape is described in the Old Testament book 'Exodus' and was a major moment in the historical relationship between God and the Jewish people. Ever since the Exodus Jewish people the world over have celebrated this as a festival. In Jesus' time Jerusalem and its Temple were the destination many Jews would visit to commemorate this event. It was also at this time that intrigue was in town. It was believed that the long awaited Messiah who was to free the Jews from foreign rule, would make his move amidst the cauldron of anticipation and spiritual fervour. The authorities were already suspicious of Jesus and His movements during the week leading up to Passover (which runs from Friday evening until Saturday evening) and this only added to their fears.

Read the Gospel of Matthew, chapter 26: His last hours.

Knowing God

In the book of Exodus God persuaded the King of Egypt, Pharaoh, to release the Hebrews by sending plague after plague. The straw that broke Pharaoh's back was the plague that killed all of the first born sons in Egypt. In this Moses was told by God to tell the Hebrews to mark their door posts with the blood of a slaughtered lamb so that the angel of death that was to bring this plague would "pass over" Hebrew homes. After the escape through the Red Sea, the principle of a sacrificial lamb to be used to deliver God's people was established in Law. The practise at certain religious times was for Jews to offer an unblemished lamb as a sacrifice to take the punishment for the owner's sin. In the ritual a priest would pray that all of the owner's wrongdoing would be transferred onto the lamb with the animal taking the punishment of death instead. Jesus became known as the Lamb of God because at Passover, He the unblemished, sinless one, laid down His life and in doing so, the sins of the world were placed upon Him. By believing and accepting Jesus' sacrifice for us we will not face the punishment for our wrongs, we can be "born again" to start afresh. What love has God for us!

Day 12

Knowing the Bible

The Bible account does not do justice to the horror of crucifixion. It was a punishment invented by the Romans that was designed to be the slowest and most painful death imaginable. It was reserved for the lowest of the low and was carried out without ceremony, sometimes with a wooden bar nailed across a tree, the victim naked and often flogged to within an inch of their life before being hung upon it. The reason Jesus was taken to the Roman Governor, Pontius Pilate, on trumped up charges, by the Jewish leaders, was because within the Empire only the Roman authorities could authorise the death penalty.

Death on the cross often took days – if thirst didn't kill you, it could be shock, blood poisoning from rusty nails or the spear of a bored guard. A way in which death was hastened was to break the legs of the crucified so that their entire body weight was taken by their outstretched arms. This ensured suffocation within minutes. Some would say that the greatest miracle of the Bible is not God's creation of the world from nothing, raising the dead or any other feat that defied nature. The greatest is that God would come in human form and suffer this.

Read the Gospel of Matthew, chapter 27: the crucifixion.

Knowing God

Jesus walked right into this punishment, but it was no accident – this was God's plan and Jesus' death was our only hope. We have been separated from God by our sin. The word 'sin' is from an ancient word meaning "missing the mark". An archer would practise at his target and if he missed it the call from the marker would be "Sin!" It didn't matter if you just missed, or missed by miles, a sin is a sin and not worthy of credit. Our sin is like that in God's eyes: whether we appear to sin by miles in practising deliberate evil or we try our best and miss the mark by a whisker, a miss is a miss. There are no points for any sin whether it is our thoughts, words or actions. God sees that the root cause of all sin is the same: we are disobedient towards God, we rebel against Him. Sin entered humanity when Adam and Eve first disobeyed God in the Garden of Eden. Since then sin has been an indelible and inescapable part of every human. This is known as 'Original Sin'. The consequence of sin is that it cost humans their place alongside God. But this separation is not just in our earthly life, it is for eternity. Our own efforts could not reconcile us with Him because it was our own efforts that got us into the mess we are in. Humans have not changed in that sense. Something drastic had to happen to break the chain of sin. Enter Jesus: the only man born whose purpose was to die.

A favourite criticism of those that attack Christianity is that it is full of hypocrites – Christians think they are better than everyone else but are actually just as bad. Neither will they let people live and let live. However, by definition, to be a Christian means to realise that you are as much a sinner as everyone else and that something drastic had to be done by God to save you. To follow Christ, you have to accept that you need saving. When you do accept this, you can be reconciled to God and saved from an eternity of being without Him.

Day 13

Knowing the Bible

A solicitor called Frank Morison decided that he wanted to investigate, using his legal training, the story of Jesus' resurrection. He was an atheist and keen to prove that Jesus did not rise from the dead. However, during the course of his work he became convinced that the Gospels were true and that Jesus had indeed risen. The gospel writers believe it happened and when you read their accounts you will notice that there is no attempt made to try and justify this belief – it is taken as a given. Further evidence of the writers' confidence in this truth is in the inclusion of women as the first witnesses to the resurrection. In the ancient world the testimony of women was not allowed in court because they were not regarded as reliable witnesses. You did not include them in a story if you wanted to claim that it was true or were out to persuade others. If you wanted to convince an audience, there were better ways than to use women. This adds a certain truth to the gospel accounts – the writers were more concerned with the truth than with doing what it took to persuade people. People have tried to find other possible explanations for the empty tomb and the missing body, but these have not stood up to scrutiny. Did Jesus recover and walk out of the tomb? Unlikely – if anyone survived the cross the specialist execution team were punished with their own lives. As a result they tended to get things done. Anyway, His resurrection appearances didn't display the awful damage that had been done to Him. Maybe Jewish leaders, fearful that the disciples would steal the body and claim the resurrection, took the body away? If so, why didn't they reproduce the body when Jesus' followers started to claim he'd been resurrected? Perhaps the disciples stole it? Well, they knew that to proclaim the resurrection would cost them their lives. Would they do this for a lie? Would you live and die for a leader who proved to be a phoney?

Read the Gospel of John, chapter 20: the disciples see Him again.

Knowing God

If Jesus had died and remained in the ground He could fairly have been described as a fraud or mad or both. Even the sensible bits of His teaching would have been discredited and by now forgotten. If He hadn't risen then His death would have been pointless. How would we know that Jesus' death dealt with our sins if He had not risen? If He didn't have power over death how could He have power over sin? Remember sin leads to death – by defeating one, Jesus showed us He had defeated the other. The resurrection proves Jesus is who He said He is. Christianity hinges on believing this truth.

What does it mean to say that death and sin have been defeated when believers still do wrong and still die? Firstly, death should have been the punishment for our sins. But because of the resurrection, believers will not face separation from God in their earthly or eternal lives. Secondly, whenever believers allow the power of God to rule their lives, then they will not sin. It is only when we go our own way that we will sin. Those who have accepted the death and resurrection of Jesus as true and essential for their lives, will want to sin less. If that happens, then what is working in them is God's supernature. We are spiritually alive if we believe in Jesus and that means we will have an eternal, spiritual life. In other words, in our earthly life the Kingdom of God lives in us, in our afterlife we live in the Kingdom of God.

Day 14

Knowing the Bible

After the resurrection, in the gospels and the first chapter of 'Acts of the Apostles' (which we will be looking at next), Jesus appeared to His disciples over forty days. We have an account here that suggests Jesus was the talk of the town. Had those in authority been able to refute the idea of the resurrection then now would have been the time. For the disciples this was obviously a time of great fear and confusion. They'd followed their leader to Jerusalem and seen Him die. Having seen their hope die they would have been astonished to see His return. Jesus had told them to wait for God's help but they did not know what form this would take. The chapter concludes with the ascension – Jesus ascends to heaven. The ascension would seem to indicate that Jesus had come from God, but He also seemed to be leaving them again. These two realisations would leave the disciples experiencing both hope and loss. Hope wins though as we depart from the Gospels tomorrow and go to the book called the Acts of the Apostles. The author of 'Acts' is also Luke and although we are not looking at the first two chapters of 'Acts' in this study, it would be worth looking at what happens between Luke 24 and our next study, Acts 9.

Read the Gospel of Luke, chapter 24: the disciples see Him again.

Knowing God

After the ascension, we are told in the first two chapters of Acts of the Apostles, that the Holy Spirit descended on the disciples. He, and 'He' is the correct term for a person of the Trinity, was able to equip Jesus' followers with the very power of God. This enabled a band of uneducated men, slow to understand Jesus, confused by events, to have the ability to teach with authority to crowds, heal, cast out demons and speak in foreign languages. Most notably at this time, known as the birth of the church, the disciples found a new courage. From a fearful huddle, these people emerged from their hiding places to go and preach the same gospel that had resulted in their leader being killed. The question remains: why would these people who had so far done their best to save their lives by remaining in hiding, now emerge to spread the word of Christ? Of the eleven male disciples that remained, only one avoided execution for spreading the good news, and he, John, was exiled to the Mediterranean island of Patmos as punishment for His work for the gospel.

The Bible teaches that the same power that raised Christ,

came to the disciples. All that worked in Him would work in them. What's more, Christians possess that same Holy Spirit today. We will see of the immense power of the Spirit told in the Bible in our coming readings, but the story of His works continues to this day. The Holy Spirit still brings people to God, giving them all sorts of abilities and strengths that in themselves they do not possess.

Day 15

Knowing the Bible

Now we leave the Gospels and go to another book written by Luke, the "Acts of the Apostles". Although Luke's Gospel tells us about the life of Jesus which happened before the events in 'Acts', many scholars believe that it was Acts that was written first. It is more of a journalistic account of what happened in the early church and the style carries the urgency of someone who was present on the rollercoaster ride that this book takes us on. Luke's use of the word "we" confirms that he was there as some of the events unfolded.

The word 'Apostle' means "one sent out". In other words, men sent by God to spread His message. The apostles were the eleven remaining from Jesus' disciples plus one. They were students (disciples) and are now messengers of what they had learnt (apostles). A twelfth was chosen to replace Judas, called Matthias.

It has been suggested that this book would be better named the 'Acts of the Holy Spirit' because the key person within it is Him. Behind all activity is the work of the Spirit, spreading the message of the Gospel like wildfire, through the apostles and other believers. Ironically, it was a Pharisee and opponent of the gospel, Gamaliel who best summed up the prospects of the church (chapter 5) when he said *"if their [apostles] purpose is of human origin, it will fail. But if it is from God, you will not be able to stop these men"*.

One of Gamaliel's students, Saul, saw things very differently. In the earliest days of the Church, the Jewish authorities fought the fire of the Spirit with a fire of its own. This fire was violence and Saul used it with the aim destroying the Christian movement. Saul appears for the first time in chapter seven as he supervises the coats of those who stoned the first Christian martyr, Stephen, to death. In today's reading Saul is sent to Damascus, a great Middle Eastern crossing point for culture and business. If the Gospel was allowed to reach that city, there would be no stopping it being carried on the winds of trade.

Read Acts of the Apostles, chapter 9: Saul's dramatic conversion.

Knowing God

There can be no other explanation for his dramatic

change than that He saw Christ on the road to Damascus. The magnitude of this will become evident when we read about his activity and writings. Saul's change introduces us to an important concept, that of repentance. Saul was brought to repentance. He was made to realise, when confronted with Christ, who he was and how wrong he'd been. However, repentance requires not just stopping dead in the tracks we are on. It also requires a change of heart strong enough to effect a complete change of direction. Saul's change could hardly be more extreme. Repentance demands an active rejection of the sins of our past and a conscious adoption of a new future. Conversion like this still happens today. For others the change of direction is a slower process and can be a bit more like watching a ship turn. But that is not wrong. The Bible says that the Spirit will work where He wills, then and today and God will complete His work in us to for His purpose. Read on to see how the Holy Spirit works in different ways in people's lives.

Day 16

Knowing the Bible

Saul, in the middle of this chapter, becomes known as Paul for the rest of our association with him. This is symbolic of his conversion and fresh start. It is also an indication of Paul's new direction which begins to unfold – Paul is the Greek version of his name, and it was to the

Greco–Roman world that Paul was to work in for most of the rest of his life. His conversion led to him taking the gospel to the Gentiles (a Jewish term meaning 'non-Jews'). This was the beginning of Paul's missionary life.

The widespread influence of the Gospel is already evident in the first verse of chapter 13. These missionaries were a real racial mixture - a Jew, Cypriot, African and an insider in the court of Herod. A convert from Herod's court would be turning their back on wealth, power and corruption. They most certainly would be endangered for such treachery but such is the power of repentance. The Herod in this passage is the son of King Herod who'd interrogated the Wise Men that had travelled to see the baby Jesus. He had ordered that the infants of Bethlehem be killed so that this Jesus could not grow up to challenge him. Herod junior, known as Tetrach, was equally depraved. Acts chapter twelve records his gruesome death. This fact is confirmed by the historian Josephus in his work 'Antiquities'. We can be confident of the truth of the Bible record because history tells us that Josephus was a Jewish defector to Rome and no friend of Christians.

Read Acts of the Apostles, chapter 13: Saul's missionary journey.

Knowing God

John, of verse 13 might be John Mark of chapter 12. This could be the author of Mark's Gospel.

In the early church is was the practice of Christians who were travelling and spreading the gospel to arrive in a new city and take the message to the synagogue, the Jewish place of worship, first. Here we begin to see the brilliance of the teaching of Paul that is further explained in his letters and which we will look at later in our study.

Paul explains Christ's credentials, describing how characters and events in Jewish history (which we will investigate later in the study) all point us towards the coming of Jesus. Jesus is the fulfilment of the history of the Jews. All of the Old Testament culminates and makes sense in the light of His work, life, death and resurrection. The history of the Jews is a little like a walk taken in hills in the countryside. The paths they took were only partly discernible to them behind and in front, the whole route never fully revealed. In coming across Jesus, the Jews were arriving at the top of the highest hill on their walk. From this point they were able to see back over their journey from the start, through the steep sections, round the bends and to the top. Jesus is the summit of their religion, the pinnacle of their faith. All of their history should now make sense in the light of the perspective that Christ gives them. This is not just something that can be applied to the Jews as a nation. It applies to us as individuals – the turns, directions, decisions and regrets that we have all make sense when we realise there is a purpose in God taking us a certain way. Who knows, you may look back and see a path revealed.

Day 17

Knowing the Bible

In all, Paul made four missionary journeys. This one and some of the other ones centred largely round what we know today as Turkey. Paul himself was from Tarsus, a town in the south-east of the country. Although Acts of the Apostles gives the impression of constant movement, these events have occurred over roughly three decades. Therefore Paul stayed in some places for a year or more at a time. That said, for the ancient world, and a dangerous one hostile to the new faith at that, such an amount of travel was phenomenal. Paul was instrumental in seeing Christianity's rapid spread. It is in the Antioch mentioned here that the term 'Christian' was first coined. Paul felt not only called by God, but to a specific role, that of taking the Gospel to the whole world. Indeed he refers to himself in the New Testament as the apostle to the Gentiles. Christ is the object of the Christian faith and He remains exalted above anyone else in Christianity as God in the flesh. However, if there are any other heroes in the religion, then Paul is probably the first of these. If ever there was an example of the power of the Holy Spirit performing amazing things through an ordinary man, this was it.

Contrast the treatment of Paul by Christians, with that of the rural community of pagans he and Barnabas encounter.

Read Acts of the Apostles, chapter 14: mission accomplished.

Knowing God

'Mission accomplished' maybe the title for today's study but a read of this chapter will not find a 'Tom Cruise' style victory. In what sense is this mission accomplished? All believers are missionaries, whether they travel to the end of the known world or across the street to a neighbour. All are expected to share the Gospel. Therefore even to say "yes" to Jesus is to, in part, accomplish the mission – it is your obedience to His call that He wants.

Paul, transformed by the Holy Spirit and the Gospel, was so determined to give both to others, that he would willingly go to his death. See how he went straight back into the city to face the same people who had just tried to kill him.

What was it that so scared the people of that city? They saw something in him that they knew would shake the very fabric of their society and challenge their way of life. We may laugh at pagan life now, but are we any better?

We may not worship statues or gods that don't exist but we do make idols of people and worship the fame and money that come with them. We then aim to shape our lives like theirs in our search for happiness. We place our faith increasingly in Tarot cards, faith healing, so-called white witchcraft, horoscopes, fate, luck, feng shui – we could go on. They are not harmless or right because they might temporarily cover over a problem or feel good. People seek answers to life's meaning in them and they become catch-alls for their problems. Alternatives to Christ may provide some comfort, relief or meaning and it is their apparent success in this which means people forget Jesus. However, they only do a partial job. Christ doesn't just tinker with our lives, He creates new people.

Day 18

Knowing the Bible

In this passage Luke starts to use "we" where previously he used "they", indicating that he had joined the mission. It should be noted that most of the earliest Christians were Jewish by birth. That meant males were circumcised. The Christian convert Timothy was circumcised because his father was not a Jew and therefore regarded as an outsider. Circumcision for Timothy was an initiation which proved his commitment to Jewish sceptics. It was a rite of passage in which a Jewish baby boy would be circumcised in the Temple or a local Synagogue. Circumcision set Jews apart from the rest of humanity physically. Therefore, the Jews were to be a people set apart, chosen for a special purpose. The mistake some Jews had made was that they believed that the act of circumcision contained within it the power to make you holy. Instead, circumcision should have been more a declaration of intent – "I have been set apart physically, now I must set myself apart to serve God in my life". Paul fell into conflict with Jewish Christians about this – he argued that circumcision was a Jewish ritual and so Gentile converts should not be forced into this. There was no power in circumcision and to demand that believers have this might turn people against becoming a Christian. Paul compromised in this situation having weighed up which of the paths would do least damage to the local church – in this instance circumcision would cause least harm to the unity of the church.

Read Acts of the Apostles, chapter 16: jailbreak in Philippi.

Knowing God

In this chapter we witness the demise of circumcision and the rise of baptism to replace it. Baptism is most commonly practiced in the West on babies and has come to be a general welcome into the Church or even into life itself if the parents are not believers. Many Churches do not baptise anyone until they are old enough themselves to decide to follow Christ. Then baptism is full immersion. This is when a believer will enter into a tank or even open water to imitate the baptism that Jesus had. The water symbolises a grave and the death of your old life. Re-surfacing represents the new life, being born again. There is no magical power in baptism – it is simply an outward sign of an inward change. Paul does not, however, say that baptism is important to being "saved", he says simply "Believe...and you will be saved". What does to be "saved" mean? It can mean being saved from your past: set free from the past mistakes that haunt you. It can also mean being saved from who you are – the personality traits that hold you down and keeps you living in guilt. But most importantly, it means to be saved from your future. That does not just mean from a future on this earth without God in it, it means an eternal life without Him. Eternity without the presence of God can only mean one place – hell. To be saved is to place your past, present and future in God's hands. In this life you get a glimmer of what that will be like in life after death. All Paul says you need to do is believe. At first this could appear as an easy way out. However, this is not some sort of wishy-washy belief that you accept in order to hedge your bets over where you will go when you die. It must be a belief that is heartfelt and involves the repentance that we studied before. When you have accepted that you need to believe in God in order to be saved, then it follows that the rest of your life must be guided by Him.

Day 19

Knowing the Bible

Paul is identified as a Roman citizen. As he was born into a Jewish family it is likely that this was a citizenship bought by his parents. This entitled you to certain rights, one of which was to take your trial to Caesar should you wish, or dare, him to hear it. It was always Paul's desire to go to Rome, the heart of the Empire, with the gospel. He would have seen the long, straight roads as the quickest way to get Christianity spread throughout the known world. Moreover, Paul was no respecter of earthly authority, not when he had been called in the way he had, and he would have revelled at the prospect of going to the highest seat of power on earth and suggesting that there was a higher one than Rome. He'd rejected the tradition of his upbringing, he had stood up to the apostles who doubted him and here we find him trying to convert a king.

Read Acts of the Apostles, chapter 26: witnessing to a King.

Knowing God

The reaction of Festus and Agrippa to Paul is perhaps more typical of how Christians are viewed in England today: slightly mad and probably harmless. Paul does not allow the authorities to dismiss him lightly and insists on taking this further – he seems almost to want to provoke the authorities so he has asked to be tried in front of someone who will take him, or more importantly, the gospel, seriously. The Roman Emperor may not intend to treat the message with more respect, but ironically to see the gospel as a threat is to in part acknowledge the power of it. There is a message for believers here in not going quietly. Paul acts with all due respect (he gestures his hand in the tradition of a public speaker of that time), uses the system as it is and does nothing to bring contempt on the message – he doesn't cause trouble. However, if Christians have been 'set apart' by God for this world then they should be visible in it making God heard and understood.

Paul is in no hurry to see himself released from his chains. He is not looking to gain credit for being a martyr – he confesses he doesn't like the chains – but he remains happy to serve in these circumstances. In the last chapter we saw Paul and companions in the dead of night, in a dungeon, singing praises to God.

In the 1970s a convicted Loyalist terrorist Billie McCurrie converted to Christianity whilst serving a life sentence for murder. He said that he felt more freedom in prison as a Christian than outside of prison before he was a Christian. Religion is often perceived as a set of rules given to control us, often to deny us pleasure. Here are two people, Paul and McCurrie, who claim greater freedom in Christ than without Him. How is this? The

Gospel of Jesus actually frees us from the laws such as circumcision and other practises that some religions place on people. However, when you are in a relationship with Jesus and one in which you are grateful for being saved from your past, present and future, you live in freedom. Imagine losing your fears, hatred, jealousy, insecurities, self-loathing, lack of purpose, dependency on substances or stimulants, need for approval. Would that not be a mental, emotional, psychological and spiritual freedom even in chains?

Day 20

Knowing the Bible

Luke's reputation as a serious historian is justified when we look at the wealth of detail he includes in this chapter. Interestingly, he doesn't separate the natural events from supernatural ones – they are woven together as a single account. Neither does he try to justify or explain his version of events. Luke is an educated medical doctor but sees no problem with this state of affairs.

Paul has assumed a role in leadership in the travelling party. Remember he began the trip as a prisoner and one who sought to serve fellow passengers and prisoners. By the end he has the Centurion following his lead and taking his counsel. That the Centurion didn't execute the prisoners is a remarkable testimony of Paul's appeal as the Roman Guards would have faced death at the hands of their own authorities for any prisoners who escaped. Paul has waited years to get to Rome and he wants nothing to get in his way now – he persuaded this Roman Guard to be sympathetic and he wanted to do the same to the Emperor himself. Rome was originally quite benevolent towards the new sect called Christianity. After all, it was seen as a non-threatening branch of Judaism, the religion of the Jews, and the Romans had absorbed them into their city quite peacefully. It is true that much Jewish rebellion existed in Israel itself, but everywhere else in the Empire that they had migrated to, the Jews were regarded as loyal members of the Empire.

This changed gradually as this radical new branch of Judaism began to attract large new followers. Christians became the enemy within, in some respects for good reason, because their beliefs were not compatible with the established order and some saw them as a threat to the very fabric of Roman rule. One of these who saw it this way was a contemporary of Paul – Emperor Nero. This most vicious and unpredictable of Emperors entertained himself variously by feeding families of Christians publicly to lions, using them as human torches in trees to light his evening dinner parties and it was Christians he falsely accused of setting fire to Rome, an act he had possibly authorised, in an attempt to divert conspiracies against his rule. It was later in his life that

Paul was to encounter the wrath of Rome.

Read Acts of the Apostles, chapter 27: shipwrecked.

Knowing God

The wonderful hymn 'Amazing Grace' is known as one that brings great peace to hearts and minds. Yet it was born out of a crisis. The author, John Newton, was converted to Christianity when, as a slave trader in the 18th century, he saw a vision of a cross during a storm at sea that he thought he could not survive. Believers can also have the peace that the Bible describes as one that "surpasses all understanding". It is a peace that, despite the storms of life, assures us that our lives are in God's hands, that He has a plan for us and that our journey has a purpose. Our ultimate destination we can be sure of, but how we get there may surprise us. Some are encouraged by Paul's example. Others look at him and are discouraged believing that they could never be like that. So why was Paul chosen by God for this? Was it his ability? See how he managed to become such a leader on this ship even though he knew nothing about seafaring. This wasn't due to his ability but to his availability. Ordinary people do extraordinary things when they make themselves available to God.

Day 21

Knowing the Bible

Reliable tradition has it that it is in Rome that Paul met his end, crucified. The book of Acts rather peters out and ends without any mention of his execution. References in other parts of the New Testament suggest Paul made another missionary journey as far as Spain before returning to Rome to suffer the persecution of the mid-60's AD under Nero. This would mean that this was not his only visit to Rome and that therefore he was released on this one.

You may find reference in the notes to verse 29 of this chapter. This is due to differences between some ancient manuscripts where the following words are missing:

(29)"After he said this, the Jews left, arguing vigorously among themselves".

It is clear that the phrase does not contradict Christian teaching or create any meaningful controversy. A few Bible scholars might get excited about whether verse 29 should be included or not but to the rest of us it is a demonstration of how the Bible has been handed down with integrity. It has not hidden its questions and because debate over such an issue still goes on, it shows how seriously experts in this field endeavour to get to the truth of this most influential and powerful of books.

Often the Bible is dismissed by those who have never looked into it as a set of myths and stories that are the work of overactive imaginations. Yet, if we are to apply the rules that historians of any kind apply to establish whether something handed down to us is a true record, we find that there is no other ancient record that gets close to the Bible for reliability. This is due to the quantity of manuscripts discovered by archaeology and the closeness of their writing to the times in question.

So much of what we take for granted in other ancient history as true, such as the life of the Roman Emperors, is based on evidence that is tiny and written centuries after the events. In contrast, the Bible has a wealth of manuscripts written in the first century after Jesus and thousands of pieces of evidence in the next few centuries which means that in volume alone it outstrips all other respected historical records by a mile. Furthermore, it is also the case that the Bible has characters such as King David, that historians previously had written off over the years as fictional creations. Archaeology has discovered evidence for the existence of these figures, Jewish and non-Jewish, in both religious and non-religious (secular) sources.

Read Acts of the Apostles, chapter 28: mission in Rome.

Knowing God

We close our study of Acts with this thought: can Christians today be like the early ones – life transforming, passionate and world changers? The key is in whose words are repeated in the last chapter – not Paul's, but the Holy Spirit's. This is not, primarily, a book about people, the apostles (despite its name), or even Paul. It is about the third person of God, the Holy Spirit. This book could be called the Acts of the Holy Spirit. The answer to our question above is this: yes, with less of us and more of Him (see John's gospel chapter 3 verse 30). It His power that raised Christ from the dead, His power that converted an enemy like Paul and His power that will raise us up.

Day 22

Knowing the Bible

Although we leave Acts, we are still with Paul, author of much of the New Testament. Acts was finished by the mid-60's AD, after much of what we are going to study now – the Epistles. A new word, but an old idea, epistle is translated today as 'letter', the common form of long distance communication. A more accurate translation of epistle may be 'postcard' given the thick nature of the paper of the time (papyrus) and the fact that envelopes were not used. In an era before emails, telephones, fast, convenient travel and even the printed word, it was by letter that an organisation stayed in communication. Paul's epistles were used and collected by the early church, which was circulated throughout the Roman Empire, to encourage and teach the believers. These churches may have had parts of the Old Testament Bible which was the Jewish Holy Book, but scripture was expensive and rare. Also, the Gospels in the complete form that we know them, were not written. Paul's letters would have been in some ways the glue that held the pioneering church together. It is with this awesome burden that he explains he is: "to preach to the Gentiles the unsearchable riches of Christ, and to make plain to everyone the administration of this mystery" the truth of which has been revealed to him.

Verse 1 suggests Paul wrote this from prison in Rome to the city of Ephesus, a place in his affections because of the three years he spent there. It was in Ephesus that Paul survived an attempt by a mob to kill him. His public challenge to the worship of Artemis, a Greek God whose image was one of the seven wonders of the ancient world and on display there, threatened the livelihood of those whose trade in idols depended on people continuing in their pagan beliefs. For this he was hunted down (see Acts 19).

Read the letter (epistle) to the Ephesians, chapter 3: Paul's ministry and prayer.

Knowing God

Paul qualifies what may appear as his arrogance in claiming to be chosen to spread the word to the Gentiles, by saying: "I am less than the least of all God's people." He is not where he is by merit but by grace. Grace is a key word in the Christian's vocabulary. Grace means a free gift that cannot be earned or deserved. There is no way that we will be good enough to earn God's favour. His nature is so utterly different from us that in our own strength we cannot possibly measure up to Him. However, rather than being abandoned by a distant God, He pours out His grace on us to give us the "freedom and confidence" (v.12) to approach Him and that He shall fill us with Himself (v.19). This is the unfathomable love of God of verse 18. Grace also reminds us that we are dependent on God and means that, like Paul, we cannot brag about who we are or what we achieve – all we have, even our faith, is a free gift from Him.

The chapter ends with Paul's powerful prayer. Prayer is an important theme in this epistle. Ephesians is best known for its last chapter in which he describes the believer as daily putting on the armour of God. This is to fight the battles that a believer faces every day. This armour is a spiritual one and often our weapon against our challenges or challengers is prayer. Prayer is necessary to receive the freedom, confidence, power and love that are described in this chapter.

Day 23

Knowing the Bible

The epistle to the Romans has been described as the Bible in miniature. This is because it is the most comprehensive of Paul's letters and clarifies Christian teaching in a single letter, better than any other book of the Bible. It includes a description of God's relationship with His chosen people, the nation of Israel, and goes on to describe how the Gospel is the good news for all nations. But there is a huge irony in this. We know from our previous readings, that Paul was desperate to reach Rome, the crossroads of civilisation and guardians of the routes that would spread the Gospel. Christianity was to become the official religion of the Roman Empire. This command was established through the might of the Empire. When the Empire was destroyed by the fifth century AD, Rome remained the centre of the Faith and could claim to be the spiritual, cultural and moral authority in Europe until the 1100's. At this time Eastern Christianity split from the West. The former became what we know today as the Orthodox Church, the West continued to be led by the Roman Church. The irony is this: by the end of the 15th century the Roman Catholic Church (as it became known) was increasingly perceived as corrupt and that it's doctrine had betrayed the original message of the Bible. A rebellion against the Roman Catholic Church began what is known as the period of the 'Reformation'. This was led by a man called Martin Luther in the 1500's. One of the inspirations for Luther's attack was the book of Romans. The city that was once seen as the key to the success of Christianity was now seen by many as the cause of its weaknesses. Furthermore, part of the challenge to the Roman Church was in the teaching of the book that bore its name.

Read the letter (epistle) to the Romans, chapter 3: Christ makes us right with God (part 1)

Knowing God

What do you want to hear first: the good news or the bad news? Often you cannot have one without the other. The same is for this topic – tomorrow is the good news, but before that must come the bad. One of the teachings of Martin Luther that challenged the Catholic Church was on 'righteousness'. The word means to be right with God or right in God's sense of being right. It is the opposite of self-righteousness which is what humans may declare to be right. It is also more than just being nice and doing good, even good that God would approve of. Righteousness belongs only to God and is a height that we cannot hope to reach on our own. We have to understand that it is God's and not ours. It also means we cannot boast of our goodness or be self-righteous. Paul describes how the nation of Israel had the very law of God at their disposal but were still destined to fail to act rightly in God's eyes. What applies to the Jews of

Paul's time and all people today is that because of our imperfect nature, we will always fall short of God's perfection. We cannot earn God's pleasure and therefore cannot earn our place in heaven. Put it this way, even when we are at our best we fall short of perfection. So how could we enter heaven, a perfect place, without ruining it? Worry not! Today is the bad news, tomorrow is the good. As a taste of the good news to come, remember that the Bible also says that it is God's will that none should perish.

Day 24.

Knowing the Bible

In the first century slavery was common practice. It may not have been as horrific a physical cause of suffering as we are familiar with in the case of Africans being transported to America. Nevertheless, the slave was still owned by someone else and legally powerless to change their situation. Slaves were traded in markets like any other commodity. Occasionally, a wealthy person out of sympathy for the slave would pay the price for a slave with the intention of once having handed over the money, setting the slave free. This buyer would be known as the slave's redeemer – they paid the price and set the captive free. Jesus Christ is often referred to as the redeemer of mankind. He paid the ultimate price to set us free from our slavery – slavery to the desire to sin, slavery to the consequences of our sin, slavery in hell when we die. There is something else we are set free from – the condemnation of God's law. That seems a strange idea, after all, are we not supposed to follow God's law? We are reminded from yesterday that it is actually impossible for us to follow God's law to His standard. The law, Paul tells us, is here to highlight for us our inability to keep it. In other words, the law is not there to help us keep on God's good side, but to show us how far short we fall of His standard. How then can we please Him? How can we be righteous?

Read the letter (epistle) to the Romans, chapter 5: Christ makes us right with God (part 2).

Knowing God

Here is the good news: we are set free from the slavery of the law. Does it mean we can behave how we want? Read chapter 6 verses 1 and 2 for Paul's reply to that. What it means is this: if we were to stand in court with the sins we have committed in our lives used as evidence against us, with God as the judge, we are doomed. We have said much already about our in-built imperfection that will result in our condemnation. The consequences of our sin will mean a poorer life on earth and hell when we die. However, this judge is like no other. In fact He is biased towards us, after all He sent His son to find us a way out of our judgement. Elsewhere the Bible describes Jesus as interceding for us, petitioning God the Father on our behalf and praying for us. You see, it is God's will that none should perish. So what was this way out of our judgement? When we appear before the Judge, as we do every day, we find that the charge sheet that should be read out is blank. The Judge has removed the charges and we stand before Him with a clean sheet of paper, new and without blemish. Our lives become a blank sheet upon which to write our new lives. How has this happened? We turned up in front of the Judge expecting a life sentence and instead got a life back. The Judge explains: someone has paid the price for you, the fine has been covered, the penalty has been paid. How? Jesus' death on the cross was the cost and the Judge's own Son paid it. This is what it means to say we have been justified – we are guilty, but counted innocent because of what Jesus did. In other words, it was Jesus who stood before His own Father as Judge and took it for us. As a result we are counted as innocent and a way has been made for us to enter heaven. Therefore, to enter heaven we must sincerely accept who Jesus is and what He did for us. Verse 1 says "we are justified by faith". This means the saving act of Christ's death is only effective if we have a genuine and heartfelt faith (trust) in the truth of this.

Day 25.

Knowing the Bible

Paul writes to address the internal rivalries within the Church at Corinth. He begs the question: what is your motive? If not love then your Church is finished.

There is only one word in the English language for 'love'. In Ancient Greek, the language of the New Testament, there are several. 'Eros', from the Greek God, was the word for romantic or sexual love and from where we get the word 'erotic'. Another was 'philia', meaning "brotherly love". This is where the nickname for the American city of Philadelphia comes from: "the city of brotherly love". There is an Ancient Greek word that made its first appearance in the New Testament. It is *agape* (pronounced "agapay"). It is the only form of love that is entirely sacrificial and gains the person showing it nothing. It is the only love possible towards your enemy. When Christ commands us to love and do good to our foes, He is not expecting that we would feel warm towards those that hurt us. Rather, it is a determination of mind to do good to them in spite of how we feel. Also *agape* love isn't biased towards those we love or like already. It is love how God loves – freely and to all, regardless of who they are.

Read the first letter (epistle) to the Corinthians, chapter 13: in praise of love.

Knowing God

You could be forgiven for thinking this God has gone soft – today we have heard about 'love' and in our culture we often associate love with softness. Yesterday we heard how God will let me into heaven just for having faith in Him. However, what do we mean when we say all you must do is have faith to be saved? Faith in Jesus is not just words, we cannot con God by saying we believe when deep down we don't. Faith isn't being 10,000 feet high in an aircraft with a parachute strapped to my back and saying I believe this would open if I jumped and then deciding to remain in my seat until the aeroplane lands. Faith is stepping out of the craft at 10,000 feet and using the parachute I said I believed in – faith demands an action. If we are not prepared to act upon what we say we believe, can we believe what we say? This is what Paul says: faith is enough but whether we really have faith is proven by whether we respond to what we believe in. Put another way, if you have been saved from an eternity in hell and given a second chance in this life, can you really respond to that with the ingratitude that does nothing? If we believe we will respond. One of these responses must be that if we have received God's amazing love then we should be willing to show it ourselves. Read verses 4-7 and exchange the word "love" with "God". John's epistle tells us that God is love, and this describes what kind of love it is. Now replace "love is" with "I am" and see how we fall short. This will remind you of our previous study on righteousness – we will always fall short in this. However, Paul is writing to believers who having accepted Jesus, should be out to demonstrate this faith. Therefore in the matter of love, we should aim to attain God's love for others. Paul describes how we see through a glass darkly, that our ways are childish and that "now I know in part". In other words, our knowledge of God's love is imperfect, lacking fullness and that until we die our love will remain faulty. However, we are urged to be seeking to reach those heights. Faith, as you can see, is not an easy option.

Day 26.

Knowing the Bible

This is another of Paul's letters written from his house arrest in Rome. The reason we have more of these from this period of his life than any other could be for two reasons. Firstly, whilst he was imprisoned letter writing might have been the only way to continue his work in support of the Church. Secondly, as the first generation of Christians were dying and Paul himself under a possible sentence of death, the Church may well have been treating the epistles with greater importance as the documents that will pass on the faith.

Philippi was another Roman outpost and the physical features that are described in the Acts of the Apostles have been unearthed by archaeology.

The Timothy mentioned in this letter crops up often throughout the New Testament and is the same person to whom Paul writes two separate letters – he seems to be Paul's protégé and a leading figure in the first century church.

We will use Philippians chapter 2 to recap ideas that we have considered before. This has more use than just to re-enforce the teaching we've studied already. It also serves to teach us that although the Bible was written by many people from different cultures, of different levels of learning (some with no formal education at all), in different eras and who never met, there is a remarkable unity of purpose in its teachings. People that know little of the Bible will argue that it contradicts itself and it would be dishonest to say that you won't find passages you will struggle with at times. However, what is more surprising is how little this occurs given that it was written over a period of maybe 1500 years, in different languages and according to some scholars, contains around forty different writers. For many, the overall beauty of the Word of God is the wonderful stream of thought and direction that characterises its teaching. It is a reassurance that God's hand was at work in directing the Bible and history.

Read the letter (epistle) to the Philippians, chapter 2: in praise of Jesus.

Knowing God

This chapter nicely pulls together several of the themes we have looked at so far:

1. The belief that Jesus and God in heaven are the same – two persons of the Trinity – is clarified from verse 6 to 11. Jesus is God but chose to submit Himself as flesh on earth to God the Father. Therefore He chose to put Himself under the Father's authority. However, they are in status equal – see that Jesus is called 'Lord' in verse 11.
2. Although the word has not been used in this study yet, a key one for believers is 'reconciliation'. This is between us and God. We were totally separated from God because of our sin, but Christ's sacrifice on the cross made it possible for us to be reconciled and enjoy a relationship with Him.
3. Follow God's example of love, putting others before ourselves, as Christ did. We are to be literally Christian, attempting to be 'Christ-like'.
4. All of our righteousness comes from Jesus – we cannot claim any credit for this.
5. We are to seek to be holy out of gratitude for God's love for us. Put another way, we are to be increasingly 'set apart' from others, shining like stars in the world.

6. The word "faith" in verse 17 refers to a belief that leads to action. Faith leads to us "working out our salvation" (verse 12) – demonstrating belief by action.

Day 27

Knowing the Bible

Did Paul really write that in verse 12? Not what you might expect in the Bible. Paul is clearly exasperated and on the attack. You can imagine the rebel Martin Luther who led the confrontation with the Catholic Church enjoying the tone and shock effect of this passage. Perhaps this book more than any other is the inspiration for the Reformation we mentioned earlier. Martin Luther often called upon Galatians in his rebellion against the Catholic Church. See chapter 2 verses 16 to 21 for a neat summary of our last few days of readings. The book explains how we are saved by faith. We are made holy (or 'sanctified') by obedient gratitude and love for the one who was sacrificed for us, and not by the good things we do.

Read the letter (epistle) to the Galatians, chapter 5: life by the Spirit.

Knowing God

In this great rousing passage there is much to draw out of it. The first is the idea of freedom in Christ. Already we have read about a prisoner who felt more freedom inside with Christ in his life than he'd had on the outside without Christ. We have also considered what freedom we can enjoy with Christ in our lives. CS Lewis said that freedom is one of the greatest gifts God has given us. Many ask why God allows us the freedom to make mistakes and choose to reject Him. But God wants a love-relationship, one where he have chosen to give our lives to Him and not because we've been compelled to. Even if He'd designed us so that we never did wrong, it would not benefit us in eternity because it is not by our behaviour that we are saved. It is by faith in Him that we are justified and therefore saved. To have faith in Him is to love Him.

Furthermore, verse 14 implores us to "love your neighbour as yourself". It is often mistakenly interpreted as avoiding actively hurting others because you wouldn't want it to happen you. For example, being polite to the beggar who asks for money, but declining to help. This is not what it means. Instead it asks us if you were that beggar, what would you want the passer-by to do for you? It is that *agape* love again. Freedom in Christ is a wonderful blessing, but it is also an awesome responsibility.

The second part describes the life we can enjoy in the Spirit. The Bible talks about the Holy Spirit as the third person of the Trinity. He, equal with the Father and Son, is our bridge to God. It is through the Holy Spirit that we experience God – the Holy Spirit in us is, literally, God in us. We have previously looked at what a life transformed by the Holy Spirit can be like. The Word teaches us that we are spiritually dead unless brought alive by the Holy Spirit. Remember how the epistle to the Romans has been called the Bible in miniature. Romans chapter 8 has been called the key chapter in this book. Read this chapter to see how the Holy Spirit saves us from spiritual death. Spiritual death in this life keeps us out of the will of God, denies us the purpose we were born for and prevents us receiving the fullness of life we could enjoy. But that loss is nothing compared to the one spiritual death leads us to when our life on earth ends.

Day 28

Knowing the Bible

Corinth, the city Paul's epistle is sent to, is an interesting place. Unlike Ephesians, this letter is aimed at this Church particularly and addresses some very specific problems. Corinth was a major seaport of the Roman Empire out of which flowed sea routes to all parts of the Mediterranean. It also brought in many cultural influences by sea from all over the world. Its reputation was much as other ports have had over the years, one of immoral behaviour, violent and sexual in nature where sailors, travellers and tradesmen were free from the constraints of home and where anything goes. The word

'Corinth' actually became a slang term for sexual immorality. At one point around 1,000 Temple prostitutes were employed in the city by pagan religious authorities. It was a place desperate for a stable Church but instead the opposite was true.

Rumours did abound in the ancient world that believers in this new faith of Christianity were cannibals. This was due to a misunderstanding of the meaning of the Holy Communion when believers eat bread and drink wine together to remember Jesus' 'Last Supper'. Add to this the secretive way Christians met in order to ensure their safety and it may not be surprising that this rumour began. There was also the suspicion that Christ's instruction to love and to live free of the Jewish law, led to behaviour that was promiscuous and immoral. We have read already of Paul's plea for the right kind of love to be the motive for the action of all believers. He spends much of the epistle trying to heal the divisions that have split the Church in Corinth several ways. It seems that sometimes the motives of the Church members were to promote their own interests and factions within it. Can we still question the inevitable failure of human nature to live rightly without God in our lives?

Read the first letter (epistle) to the Corinthians, chapter 15: the afterlife.

Knowing God

We began our look at the New Testament with a birth, so it seems right to conclude it by looking at death, or rather what we will find after death. Today, just as in Corinth, people have questioned whether there can be life after death because they question what part of us it is that survives death. If our soul isn't in physical form how can it go to an actual place called heaven? Or, if heaven is a spiritual place, how could my physical self go there? Paul's answer fits in with the gospel message that those who believe in Jesus become new creations. In our death we are recreated into a heavenly body – we will be us, but not as we know it! Not so hard for the creator of the universe to do surely?

Read verse 17 and consider this: It has been the case that prominent figures in the Church in recent years, have questioned the physical resurrection of Christ. They have revised the resurrection to being not so much an event witnessed by Christ's followers, as a psychological turning point where their hope has some how been restored after Christ's death. That is to deny the power of God and the life transforming effect of the gospel. Resurrection for Christ and us is possible to a miracle working God. The resurrection is God's victory over sin and death and it is essential to believe in this so that we can be new creations now and into eternity.

Day 29.

Knowing the Bible

Like a film that flashes back midway through we leave the New Testament and go back to the Old. As with all flashbacks, by going back in time the present starts to make more sense. We began with Jesus in the Gospels because it is Him that the faith revolves around. It was He who inspired the rest of the New Testament and He who fulfils the promises and teachings of the Old Testament. The Old Testament remains absolutely relevant to us today because it teaches us of the character of God and His people's struggles to live in a relationship with Him. In fact, the word 'Israel', which is the name of God's chosen people, means "struggles with God". ('El' is the Hebrew word for God – anyone with a name that ends in 'el' has a name of Hebrew origin). For a Christian there can be no greater endorsement for the Old Testament than the fact that Jesus quoted it. He was, of course, a Jew and steeped in the holy book. We will see in later studies how Jesus fulfilled the prophecies and teaching of the Old Testament.

Read Genesis, chapter 1: the beginning of everything.

Knowing God

Genesis means "origin". In the last century and a half, the book of Genesis has been under attack. New scientific theories about the origin of the universe have emerged that have become the unquestioned orthodoxy. However, it may surprise readers to learn that by science's own definitions of what is proof, these theories remain precisely this, unproven theories. All those believers in a solely scientific explanation for the origin of the universe have to exercise something normally associated with the religious – faith. "I'll believe it when I see it" is a reason often given for not believing in God. Yet when it comes to scientific alternatives, people will accept without serious questioning what they are told. This is without handling the evidence themselves or seeing with their own eyes, let alone understanding what they are told. The only difference between a scientific believer and a religious believer is that they put their faith in different authorities. One theory of the 'Big Bang' is that in the beginning there were gases that reacted to cause the universe to begin. We can't say they were somewhere, because nowhere existed. Nor can we say how they got there or how long they were there because time itself did not exist. They were minute in size and spontaneously exploded. Within a tiny fraction of a second this explosion had expanded to form a universe millions of miles wide. Out of these gases came all that was needed to later form all solid material and life that we see in the universe today. If this is true it requires faith to believe it. To a Christian, it might appear that those who follow the scientific faith put their hope in the imperfect ability of man to provide them with answers. For Christians faith is in the perfect God. Furthermore, we do Genesis an injustice if we look at it as a textbook about how the universe began. It is a book rich in deeper truths about what it is to be human and our relationship with God. Put your faith in this authority and discover proof of another kind – that God is real and living in you: a truth far greater than a mere fact. Jesus trusted in the authority of the Bible and it proved true in His life.

Day 30

Knowing the Bible

You will notice that the title describes a man called Abraham, but here your Bible refers to him as Abram. It is the same man. To see where the name changes read chapter 17. 'Abram' means "Exalted Father", 'Abraham' means "Father of many". Chapter 12 marks a major event in the Bible. Here a man is called by God out of a land which is today called Iraq. Before now no such thing as a nation of God's people existed. If you are interested in going back, we have already passed Adam and Eve, Cain and Abel, Noah and the Flood, and the Tower of Babel – all great Bible stories. It is here, however, that God calls the man who would come to be regarded as the Father of Judaism. Abram is sent into the land of Canaan and introduces the region to something new to the people – monotheism. That is, belief in one God rather than many which was the practice of the time. We are already familiar with Canaan under other names: Israel or Palestine. Canaan was the name of the people which occupied the land that was eventually overtaken by the Hebrews (the early name for the Jews), the chosen nation of God. This is our first encounter with the land that dominates Bible history. In fact, this small tract of land, which is approximately the size of Wales, is today still fought over by Jews and Muslims, and seems to be central to much of the other conflict in the world.

Read Genesis, chapter 12: God calls Abraham.

Knowing God

Notice the deal God did with Abram in verses 1 – 3. Firstly He calls for Abram's obedience and then He promises to bless Abram as the Father of a nation that doesn't yet exist. This kind of deal is known as a 'covenant'. God makes many in the Bible and they are two-way promises that guarantee great blessing to those who are obedient to Him. It is not that God needs us to make deals with Him, but that obeying Him is actually in our own interest. It is like a parent who insists that a child carries out their wishes – it is not for the sake of the parent that the instruction is given, but for the child. If the child follows they will enjoy rewards and be safe.

The words 'testament' which we give to both parts of the Bible, Old and New, mean 'covenant'. Both 'testament' and 'covenant' mean in modern English, 'promise'. In other words, the Old Testament is the old promise or covenant between God and His people. The New Testament is when Jesus fulfils the promises of God and makes a final and 'new' covenant. That covenant is that if we obey Jesus, as Abram followed God's call, we too will enjoy enormous blessing. We may not Father a nation, but we will enjoy being one of God's children and have the promise of future life with God. No matter how great Abraham appears as the Father of a nation, his heritage is earthly, historical. For us, the amazing grace of God means that even in our own historical insignificance, our inheritance is even greater – it is not earthly but eternal. Our inheritance, and the promise, testament and covenant of Jesus is that we have access to a kingdom. Not a kingdom of this world, but God's very own.

Day 31

Knowing the Bible

The book of Genesis covers a period known to Jews and Christians as the period of the Patriarchs, the fathers of the faith. Abraham, Isaac and Jacob are referred to in the same breath in the Bible and two of them are in today's reading.

Increasingly, archaeology is vindicating the era of the Patriarchs as historically true. It became fashionable in the study of the Old Testament to question the traditional view that the life of the Patriarchs actually happened. Instead, it was asserted by twentieth century scholars that these stories were written just a few centuries before the life of Christ, rather than over a thousand years, which the Bible indicates. However, archaeology has established that some of the stranger cultural practices of the time that were believed by many to be fictional, actually did exist. For example, the way trading was carried out during this period, is described in detail in Genesis. This way of doing business has been confirmed by independent historical research.

Read Genesis, chapter 22: Abraham and Isaac.

Knowing God

Before God's people could rule, they had to learn to be ruled. Here Abraham goes on a painful journey learning this. Part of the promise (covenant) God had made with Him was that if Abraham obeyed Him and moved to Canaan, God would bless Abraham and his wife Sarah with many children. This was at last realised in very old age and Abraham would have felt His obedience was rewarded. However, God reminded Abraham that, unlike your paid job, you cannot retire from God's work – when you agree to His terms your life belongs to Him. For many today that is too much to ask. For others it is of great comfort to know that responsibility for their lives is passed onto the One who designed them, loves them more than anyone else and who knows better than anyone else what is good for them. Abraham chose the latter course and because of this, what a legacy he left. We may never see or know the future we create if we choose to obey God – that is His responsibility. If we hand our life to Him with all the benefits that brings, then we must be prepared to trust our future to Him as well.

I mentioned that Abraham, Isaac and Jacob are the first three generations of what was to become the nation of Israel. Israel was the name that God chose for Jacob and you will remember that it means 'struggles with God'. Obedience to God is the struggle we face because of the first sin of Adam and Eve. Adam and Eve disobeyed God because they wanted to rule over their own lives which is why they ate from the tree of the knowledge of good and evil. We, like Abraham, Isaac and Jacob, have to learn to let God be the ruler of our lives – just compare Adam and Eve with the Patriarch's to see the difference between the futures we can leave for our descendants.

Day 32

Knowing the Bible

Having been called by God to Canaan, the last of the Patriarchs had moved to Egypt because of famine (it is from this part of the Bible that we get 'Joseph and the Amazing Technicolour Dreamcoat'). Whilst in Egypt, the

Hebrews became slaves under the three consecutive Kings called Rameses, whom archaeology confirms were Pharaohs in the second millennium BC. Moses, famously was discovered in a basket in the bulrushes having been hidden from Pharaoh who feared the number of Hebrews in his kingdom and had ordered the slaughter of their first born. Ironically, Moses was discovered by Pharaoh's daughter and he grew up in the royal court. However, into adulthood, he eventually realised that he was a Hebrew and that by remaining within the ruling family, he was helping to oppress his own people. He murdered an Egyptian guard who was attacking a Hebrew at work and as a result went on the run. In chapter 3 we read that after Moses' forty years of exile in the wilderness, God appears to him, calling him to set his people free after 400 years of slavery. The book of Exodus, or 'the escape', is the account of the ten plagues sent by God to bring about their freedom. Chapter 12 tells of the Hebrew flight for freedom back into the land promised them through Abraham generations before. I strongly recommend a read of Exodus chapters 13-14 to get the full account of the escape.

Read Exodus, chapter 12: Moses encounters God.

Knowing God

In chapter 12 we have the Hebrew escape: Pharaoh, tormented by the ten plagues God sent in order to 'persuade' him, eventually agrees to let the people go. It is an incredible story because in this most significant part of Jewish history, we find striking parallels with the life of Christ. These lead us to conclude that Jesus was the fulfilment of what is known and taught in the Old Testament. For example, in the Exodus when God sends the angel of death to kill the first born sons of Egypt, the Hebrews are commanded to sacrifice and spread the blood of an unblemished lamb around their doorposts to alert the angel to 'pass over' their homes and leave their children safe and well. In the New Testament Christ became the lamb whose blood rescued people – He was unblemished because he was sinless and in His death His people were saved. In Exodus we find the origin of the Passover festival which is the meal Jesus was celebrating at the Last Supper. During the Exodus the Jews took bread for the journey. It was this that Jesus broke on the night He was betrayed. Lastly, the escape was a setting free of the people from slavery to the Egyptians. The slavery that Jesus set people free from was sin. This means that by accepting His death for our sins, we are free from them. Does this mean that those who believe in Jesus no longer sin? Well, the idea is that by the power of the Holy Spirit we will increasingly become like Jesus and increasingly lose the desire to sin. However, we are not Him or ever will be, so in what sense are we free from sin? As well as being free from the constant desire to sin we are free from the consequences of our sin. From Adam and Eve onwards the consequence of our disobedience has been separation from God in this life and the next. In the next life separation is even more serious – it means an eternity without Him, in another word, hell. Christ frees us from the chains of hell.

Day 33

Knowing the Bible

As part of the Hebrew Exodus there is the famous crossing of the Red Sea. After releasing the Hebrews, Pharaoh has a change of heart and ordered their recapture. In the pursuit, God's people become trapped between the sea and the army. God commands Moses to raise his staff and the sea parts for them to cross. It then closes behind them destroying the Egyptian army. This has been interpreted as a kind of baptism for the Jews (although they didn't get wet), symbolising the passing of the old life and the beginning of a new one. After this, the Hebrews go into the desert and head back for the land first promised them, Canaan, through Abraham. This should have been no more than a two week trek but actually took them 40 years. This was due to their disobedience and, despite what they had witnessed, their lack of faith. They were unable to return to Canaan until they had accepted God's rule and were prepared to live as God's people should. God had first appeared to Moses when he was 80 in the wilderness. He remained God's representative to the people for another 40 years but himself died before the Hebrews could enter the

Promised Land. In this time Moses had tried to lead them to obedience and the passage for today describes the famous 10 Commandments that are still part of the moral foundation of Jews and Christians.

Read Exodus, chapter 20: a summary of God's law.

Knowing God

The 10 Commandments place first the importance of acknowledging God. Jesus did this when He was asked in the gospels what was the most important commandment. To some this makes God look like a jealous being, one who enjoys attention. However, let us remember that God existed before even the universe – He does not need us. We are called to put Him first because it is in our own interests to do so. If we do that, we can know our own maker's will for us - He is our designer and knows what is best for us. Therefore we need to get to know Him in order for us to live the life he has planned for us. Another criticism levelled at religion is that it is all about following impossible rules. That said, many people today would agree that most of the 'Ten' have stood the test of time. Furthermore, there is another way in which we can look at these ten commands. It is true that we are expected to try and keep them. However, when read from a believer's perspective, the emphasis in the commands change. Jesus taught, and the first commandment suggests this, that if you love God with everything, then all other moral behaviour will naturally follow. It means that when your love for God is strong and the Holy Spirit is actively involved in your life, the ten rules stop being an impossibly hard standard to reach. Instead they start to become a reality. For example, the commandment "You shall *not* steal" means that when you love God with all your heart, "You *shall* not steal". In other words, you will not have the desire to steal, you will not want to do wrong. Not because you are commanded, but because you do not want to hurt the God you love. The power of God's love can change our heart's desires and make lives like that. When our obedience is based on this love for Him rather than fear, following His laws stops being a burden and becomes our desire. In other words "You shall not..." stops being a command to do something and becomes a confirmation of what you are doing.

Day 34.

Knowing the Bible

Here we leave the collection of the first five books of the Bible. These are sometimes called the "books of Moses" due to the tradition that he wrote them. If you are Jewish the five are called the "Torah". This means 'Law' or 'Instruction'. The first five books consist of the commands of God given to the Hebrews up to and including the life of Moses, of which the Ten Commandments are a part of this. At the end of the five books, the Hebrews are poised on the east side of the River Jordan, waiting for the command to go take the land. It is here that Moses dies (Deuteronomy 34). Like a soap opera cliff hanger, we need the next episode to see whether, at last, the people will finally conquer the land first given through Abraham. Now they are led by one of Moses' most loyal lieutenants, Joshua. It is the turn of the children of the covenant to inherit what God promised them.

The famous conquest of Jericho takes place in what archaeologists think is the oldest known city on the planet. Interestingly, recent excavations have unearthed remarkable evidence of a catastrophe that caused the walls of the city to collapse. Jericho remains a hotly contested piece of land.

You will notice reference to "the ark" in verse 4. This is not to be confused with Noah's Ark which was the boat constructed to save Noah, his family and animals when God sent a flood to cover the earth. This is the ark of the covenant. If you have ever seen the film "The Raiders of the Lost Ark", you may know that it is about this very object. We know from previous study that the word 'covenant' means a two way promise between God and His people. In the 'ark of the covenant' was kept the original stone tablets of the Ten Commandments. From the film you may remember the chest-like box that was the ark. It is described like this in incredible detail in the Bible. The ark has been of fascination not just to the fictional Indiana Jones but to genuine archaeologists because of it's unaccounted for disappearance later in the Bible. From a position of centrality in the faith of the people (notice that it is held in the middle of the people in the conquest of Jericho) it just ceases to be mentioned later in the Old Testament. It is strange that given its importance, there is no account of how it went or even what a loss it was.

Read Joshua, chapter 6: the battle of Jericho.

Knowing God

The number seven appears frequently in this chapter. Seven is symbolic of perfection, but there is nothing magical or lucky about the number itself. Notice how meticulously Joshua and the Israelites (Hebrews) follow God's instructions. You could say that they were perfect in their obedience. It was by this obedience that the walls of the fearsome city of Jericho came tumbling down. Joshua was a great leader, fearless of men but submissive to God. Look at the last three verses of chapter five – see that he fears no man, but when he realises the figure was an angel from God, he falls down in reverence. The commander-in-chief had learnt that the first step to victory is to put yourself second in command. The walls of Jericho remind us of the barriers that the world puts up to the Christian message, whether they be in society in general or individuals who reject or mock it. However, God honours our stand for Him and will be with us in all our battles.

Day 35

Knowing the Bible

We pass through history now to King David, probably Israel's most famous king. After Joshua died the Israelites struggled to obey God and blundered their way to a partial conquest of the Promised Land. Following Joshua was the period known as the time of the Judges, when God sent leaders to guide and teach the people in God's way. As God was supposed to be their Lord, the Israelites did not have a king. However, they blamed many of their failures on the lack of a king so God eventually allows one. The first was Saul, who himself was very flawed. The second was David who began life as a shepherd boy. Yet another figure in the Bible called from humble origins to lead powerfully, serving as a great encouragement to believers today. The enemies in this story are the Philistines and it was over these that the Israelites failed to conquer due to their disobedience. It is from 'Philistia' that we get the word 'Palestinian', a word used to describe people of the region today. Still, the land is hotly contested, as we see in this story, and still the claim to the land is broadly between those who want to call it the Promised Land of God, the land named after the patriarch who became known as Israel; and those who want to call it Palestine and who have their own claim on it.

Read the first book of Samuel, chapter 17: David's victory over Goliath.

Knowing God

The modern image of the shepherd as a fatherly, devoted servant is much to do with the image that has developed over the years of Jesus as a gentle, kind and wise man. Jesus called Himself the Good Shepherd and He is often painted gazing lovingly and cosily at a sheep or flock. We have seen from early in our study that is far from the whole story with Christ and it is far from true of the ancient art of shepherding. They were people who were dishonoured because they were away from home for long periods and so unable to protect their wife's honour. They were also seen as thieves of other's pasture in parched landscapes. David was one of these, and like Jesus, attended to his work with bravery (it was a perilous job) and a servant heart, minding not what people made of him. Contrast this with the fearsome figure of Goliath, whose size is a metaphor for all the challenges we encounter in our Christian life that seem too big to overcome. These could be struggles with addiction, sexual matters, materialism, pride, fear of admitting you are a Christian, managing to conduct yourself in a godly way in the workplace, controlling anger to name just a few. In verse 8 Goliath called the Israelites to fight in the name of Saul, their king.

However, a worldly reason for meeting their challenge was not enough to motivate them. Today, sometimes we find that doing what is right is hard when the motive is that it is for our own good or the good of others. David put it into a different perspective - he was not motivated for his own good or that of his fellow Israelites, but because the authority of his God was challenged. If we are true servants of God we will stand up to face the challenges in our lives that can make our walk so difficult. It reminds us of the first commandment – that of loving God and that by following this, all else will follow. Instead of a burden, our obedience to God will be our desire. Like Joshua, David feared no man and took the command to put God first, literally. Do that and see your Goliaths fall and enemies flee.

Day 36

Knowing the Bible

Samuel was a prophet who was involved in the appointment of David as king. The name itself means "hearer of God". The books themselves were written after the time of David's famous son, Solomon, the king of great wealth and wisdom. This would place it as after 930BC. This would make David's rule around one thousand years before Jesus came. He had, as king of Israel, helped the people conquer the long sought after city of Jerusalem. It was of strategic importance for the region, situated as it is on a hill overlooking the nation. It was also known as 'Zion' and those today still committed to maintaining and extending the nation of Israel carry the label 'Zionist'. Jerusalem had been inhabited by the Jebusites who had managed to hold the city against attacks for generations. They were compromised, not by an onslaught of a large army, but by a secret raid up the water shaft that supplied this city on the hill. Only by such an attack could the fortress city be taken. As a result of the conquest, Jerusalem also became known as the 'city of David' and he extended the fortress to turn it into the dominant city of the region for years to come (see chapter 5). Incidentally, the water shaft was excavated by archaeologists in the twentieth century. However, this conquest did not put paid to enemy attempts to capture Jerusalem. David's son, Solomon, built the first Temple at Jerusalem that became one of the wonders of the ancient world. This was later attacked on successive occasions before being destroyed by invaders still seeking control over this strategically important location.

Read the second book of Samuel, chapter 11: David's sin.

Knowing God

It was from this great city that David committed a very great crime which we read about here. You might expect that a man who, by following his God, has risen from shepherd boy to powerful king, would out of gratitude ensure that his behaviour reflected one so privileged. I have asserted that when you love God you will desire to serve Him and do as He would expect. Yet here is a man magnificently blessed by God who not only fails to control his basest instinct, but in fact makes matters worse by weaving a tangled web of deceit to cover his tracks. This is not a reflection on the power of God or the truth of His ways. It is a reflection on human nature and the gulf between us and God. That difference is summed up in the word 'holiness'. Holiness is a key concept in Christianity and in one word describes the moral character of God. He is holy, perfect in His ways. We are not expected to achieve this but the point is that we should be seeking holiness, to live according to God's way, not seeking the temptations of the world. David tried to serve God and his own desires and as a result his life became a terrible mess. Holiness cannot be achieved this way. For us, holiness is separation from worldly temptations. Holy living is for God's sake because it honours Him and shows our gratitude to Him for what He has done for us. It is for our own sake because it leads us to avoid the temptations that can ruin our own lives, or at least stop us wanting the things that ultimately don't bring us happiness or fulfilment. Holiness is also for the sake of others because a holy life is one that will stand out. If we stand out for God, others will notice and enquire about the God who has made us new creations.

Day 37

Knowing the Bible

Welcome to the Psalms (pronounced *'sarms'*). These remain a great comfort and encouragement to many believers today. They are used to provide strength, prayers and songs. One of the famous is Psalm 23 from which we get the well-known hymn 'The Lord is my Shepherd'. Written as songs of praise, they have been used that way by worshippers ever since. Many of them were written by King David and speak of the struggle of a man in his relationship with his God. They beautifully describe the high points and touchingly express the low times. The Psalms remain for many Christians their favourite book of the Bible because although a lot of them are one man's account of his spiritual journey, it describes the experience of every Christian throughout the ages. If you want to know how it feels to be a Christian, read David's cries for help, of joy, success, pain, and failure. In fact, if you get to know the life of David, you may be able to work out at what times of his life he wrote certain Psalms. They are a kind of spiritual autobiography. The Psalm we are looking at today is written following the affair we read about yesterday. This was penned after the prophet Nathan had visited David and challenged him for his wrongdoing.

Read Psalm 51: David's prayer of repentance

Knowing God

A few years ago a Christian minister went to a conference of world religions and the question was asked of the delegates "what is it that makes your religion different from the others?" The minister replied "forgiveness". It is true that, unlike other religions, Christianity places that at the heart of the faith. The reason it is so central is that God is so holy and we're so fallen that there appears an unbridgeable divide between us. This means that without forgiveness we cannot enjoy a relationship with Him - we are estranged from our Father.

Furthermore, unlike other religions who believe you can earn a place in heaven, Christians believe that we do not have the ability to work our way into heaven. Amazingly, His forgiveness is inexhaustible as long as our regret is sincere. That means there is no-one, no matter their past, who cannot receive God's forgiveness. If David could be forgiven after what he did, then so can all of us.

My own conversion to Christianity came in my bedroom one night when, as a non-believer and after much soul-searching, I asked God to make Himself known to me. What came was firstly a sense, like David, of my guilt and then an overwhelming presence of forgiveness that washed away my past and broke down the barrier that had stopped me from coming to know Him. From that moment on I knew I was His child and that life would never be the same again. The baggage of shame I carried with me was offloaded. I found I could have a relationship with a loving God who was interested in me personally and who had a plan for my life. I was reunited with Him, my relationship with Him had begun.

Day 38

Knowing the Bible

This triumphant chapter confirms in the Israelite's eyes that God, who is ruler of the universe, is also their Lord. This Temple, whose dimensions and interior made it one of the wonders of the ancient world, became the symbol of God's provision for them. His greatness had established Israel as the power in the region. It took seven years to build. The impact on Jewish minds was to give them not only a permanent home in Jerusalem, but also an eternal one. The Temple was to be God's seat on earth. The journey into the Temple symbolised a journey into His presence. The Temple inside had various sections to it. The further you got in, the closer to God's presence you became. The innermost area was the Holiest of Holies which was separated from the rest of the Temple by a thick curtain. This curtain represented the sin that separates us from God. Only the High Priest could enter here. It was him that on one day a year entered the Holiest of Holies to perform a sacrifice for the sins of the whole nation. This was called the Day of

Atonement. As the Holiest of Holies was supposed to contain the real presence of God, the High Priest was seen as most likely to be the purest and stand before God. He would enter the room sprinkled with the blood of the lambs, sacrificed for the sins of the people. The High Priest would go beyond the curtain to offer the blood and prayers as an atonement for our sins. By this act we would be justified and the penalty paid for our sins.

Read the first book of Kings, chapter 8: the Dedication of Solomon's Temple.

Knowing God

Again we see this idea of the holiness of God as distinct from humans. So much so, that only one soul, the High Priest, could approach His presence according to the Jewish Law. The High Priest carried the sacrifice of the people. However, what Jesus revealed was that the High Priest himself could not be sinless and therefore the sacrifice would not be sufficient. Jesus solves the problem of requiring a sinless High Priest. Firstly, Jesus was the only one that could be the sacrifice because He is God's sinless son. Secondly, priests are mediators between God and humanity. Jesus describes Himself as that mediator. He said in the gospels that He would return to heaven to pray forever for us to the Father. In becoming our High Priest, Jesus broke down the barrier of sin between us and God that the curtain in the Holiest of Holies represented. In fact, in the gospels the curtain Temple is described as being torn when Jesus died (see Mark chapter 15). In other words the barrier of sin that separated us from God was gone. Because of Jesus we no longer need a special day in the year or a certain technique to speak to God – the curtain of sin has gone and we can go by prayer directly into the presence of the living God.

Day 39

Knowing the Bible

The King at this time was Ahab, which is well attested by non-Jewish historical records and Elijah was one of the great prophets of the Old Testament. A prophet is someone who is a messenger from God. The messages they bring vary in style: some foretold of events that would happen and required our action. Sometimes the prophet brought a message from God that expressed His pleasure or displeasure. Prophets were Israel's conscience. Messages were for individuals, groups or the nation. Prophecy is not predicting the future; it is communicating God's plan and purpose. One purpose of God and Elijah's cause was to fight the worship of false gods. This was a constant battle in Israelite history from Genesis and into the New Testament. In this passage we encounter Baal, a false god worshipped in the region by cultures that lived amongst the Israelites. Baal was characterised by the worship of idols and statues. The use of man-made 'props', that became worshipped themselves, was forbidden by Jewish religion because it wasn't the true God that was being worshipped.

Read the first book of Kings, chapter 18: Elijah and the pagan prophets.

Knowing God

As discussed before, we may like to think of ourselves as above worshipping idols. The popularity of media that elevates people to celebrity prove that this is not the case. What is strange to a believer today is not the worship of an invisible God, but that we seem to worship humans. At least if the God of the Bible does exist He is worth worshipping. We know how imperfect humans are, but yet we worship them. 'Worship' is by definition giving something what it is worth. Worship, if you believe in Jesus, is about giving Him what He is worth, which is giving Him your life. The worship of Baal seems bizarre to us. However, consider the worship of professional footballers we practice today. We dress in clothes to match the players, flock devotedly to the temple (stadium) each week. We sing and dance to tell of their greatness, even when they're not, and then for the rest of the week talk about the match, spreading the good news, trying to convert people (even if it is good humouredly), waiting expectantly for the next game when we will go religiously through the ritual of it all again. Some will even fight, risking their health and possibly their lives for the honour of players who probably are not from the town or city they are playing for and who would leave to join another team at the drop of a hat if a better offer came along. There is nothing wrong with sport, music or many other interests and forms of entertainment. It becomes idolatry when the interest becomes the focus of your life and distracts you from giving Jesus what He is worth. Often I have conversations with people who laugh at Churches where the worshippers outwardly express their excitement about God. These believers communicate with Him as if He is there with them and express gratitude for who He is and what He has done. I ask the mockers to compare that devotion with the object of their worship, be it football, a pop group or any other kind. The reply is often that "at least my object is real". True, but if my God is real, which is the one worthy of my devotion? Surely there is no comparison? Becoming a Christian involves a change of perspective. These things we enjoy are part of life, but only one is worthy of our worship.

Day 40

Knowing the Bible

As you know, the Old Testament begins with the five books that make up the Jewish Law. After that come the History books, of which we have looked at Joshua,

Samuel and Kings. There are the poetic books: Psalms, Lamentations and Proverbs. Then there are the prophetic works, each book written by a single prophet. There are the three major prophetic books, Isaiah, Jeremiah and Ezekiel and there are the minor ones of which Amos, our book today, is one. The label 'major' and 'minor' are to do with the length of the books and not their importance.

You may remember back to our earlier look at the Patriarchs. Abraham had Isaac, he in turn had Jacob (whose name was changed to Israel) and he had twelve sons, the most famous being Joseph with that coat of many colours. Out of each of these twelve sons grew a tribe that made up the nation of Israel. This maybe the reason that Jesus chose twelve disciples many centuries later: as a sign of His fulfilment of the history of Israel and to signify the birth of a new kind of kingdom. These twelve tribes existed as one nation until the tenth century BC.

By the time of Amos and the other prophets, the nation had split into two. The seed of this problem was sown by Solomon. He is often remembered for his great wisdom and wealth but late in his reign he turned to idol worship and took many wives, something forbidden because the Jewish faith had tried to end polygamy in the region. There were winners and losers under Solomon and rebellion began to emerge led by Jeroboam. At Solomon's death Jehoboam commanded ten of the twelve tribes against Solomon's heir and new king, Rehoboam. The rebellion was successful which brought the end of the unified monarchy and destroyed the structure of the Jewish nation. The ten tribes of the north became known as Israel, the two in the south, Judah. These two separate states existed until the sixth century BC.

Read Amos, chapter 4: a warning against persistent sin.

Knowing God

Here Amos is attacking the arrogance and disobedience of the nation. It is interesting that Israel was the author of its own destruction. Before it split, Israel had become strong and independent, which possibly explained why its leaders forgot God. In our society of great material wealth it is common to hear that "I don't need God". People associate faith with neediness. Before coming to faith in Christ I believed that. It wasn't until I realised who He was, that it put who I was into perspective. Then I knew that I needed Him in order to have His plan as my purpose; His new life, instead of my old one. Eternal life in His presence, rather than eternity separated from Him. In that sense there is nothing wrong with neediness – we were designed to need God – there is a 'god-shaped hole' in all of us. Humans need relationships and it is better to rely on one with Him than one with the bottle, money or even people. Despite the apparent 'neediness' of Christianity, it has also been the inspiration for centuries for great achievements in government, art, architecture, literature and inspired ordinary people to perform courageous acts that have changed the world. Two famous examples are William Wilberforce's campaign to end slavery and Martin Luther King's leadership of the Civil Rights Movement in America. Israel achieved more with God than without Him. Wilberforce and King recognised this.

Day 41

Knowing the Bible

Isaiah is writing, like Amos, during the time of the divided kingdom. He is regarded by many as the greatest of the written prophets for two reasons. Firstly, much of his prophecy of a future Saviour being born from the line of David, was fulfilled when Jesus was born. These verses are recalled at carol services.

Secondly, he describes to us the full range of God's plan for His people: the provision for them, their rejection of Him; His punishment of them and finally His sending of a saviour. God's judgement and salvation are beautifully painted for us. Without going into the detail of Hebrew language, Isaiah is without equal in the Bible – he can truly and technically be described as a poet.

Read Isaiah, chapter 40: God's words of comfort.

Knowing God

It is apt that in nearing the end of our study we find ourselves having come almost full circle. On reading chapter 40 you may find in verse 3 a hint of the Gospel, where we began. John the Baptist, in prophesying the imminent arrival of the Christ, talked about preparing a way for the Lord. This is a wonderful chapter that reminds us of who we are in comparison to God and tells of a coming saviour who restores us. We are left in no doubt as to who judges us and who saves us – this theme is current throughout Isaiah. Although I hope this study has answered some people's questions, if you are anything like me, the study itself will have raised even more questions for you. Two things that I struggled with when I converted were questions around salvation and judgement. For example, is there a certain amount of faith in God I must have in order to be saved? In other words, do I have to live every minute conscious of Him being with me and if I fail in that, do I lack the faith to go to heaven? With regards to judgement, what happens to those who never heard about Jesus before they died – do they go to heaven or hell? I raise these not because I can answer them easily or because I want to create doubt in people's minds. Christians have to face up to these issues. I came to a place of peace about such difficult questions when, like Isaiah, I put God in charge of the answers. It is so tempting, especially in an age of scientific achievement, to think that as humans we should be able to work out the answers to everything. This is why people often won't believe – they demand all the answers, not realising who it is they are demanding them from. To use Isaiah's word, I "comforted" myself with this: that being able to decide who is saved and how we are judged and why, would be a dangerous in the hands of man. We have proved ourselves incapable of using wisely the gifts we have been given, such as free will. It is good that responsibility for judgement and salvation are in God's hands and not ours. In fact, rather than seeing my failure to understand or know the answers to these questions as a cause for concern or a weakness in Christianity, I came to see it as a strength. For me, it was reassuring to have a God that was in control of all things, that these were responsibilities kept from me for my own sake. After all, that was why Adam and Eve were forbidden to eat from the tree of the knowledge of good and evil – we cannot handle such fruits well. All I need to know to avoid judgement and attain salvation is the saviour Isaiah foretold us about.

Day 42

Knowing the Bible

At the age of 13, Daniel was taken into captivity by the Babylonians, the empire now in modern day Iraq. He was not alone – he was part of the historical event known as the Exile. After the Exodus, the Exile is the most significant event in Jewish biblical history. Whereas the Exodus gave Judaism a hero in Moses, a hope and reacquainted them with their God, the Exile left them defeated, feeling that the nation and all hope was gone, and abandoned by God.

The divided kingdom of Israel had weakened itself. As a result the Babylonian forces were able to lay siege to and conquer Jerusalem. The term 'Exile' refers to the fleeing of many Jews abroad and the capture of a few thousand Jews to serve the Babylonian king Nebuchanezzar. The Temple was ransacked and desecrated. Despite the division of the Jewish people, they all felt the loss of their spiritual home and for a while it felt God had abandoned them. The violation of their city, which God had promised to protect, and the trauma for those that were forced to leave, caused a crisis of identity in the Jewish people. They adopted the cultures of the new places they found themselves in, intermarrying with them and compromising the faith of their fathers.

However, whilst some Jews remained physically in Jerusalem, a remnant of those in exile remained in Jerusalem spiritually, culturally and psychologically. They'd always intended to return. Eventually they did, when the Babylonians were themselves conquered by a new power in the region, the Persians (modern Iran – things never change).

Eventually the Persians decided to release the Jewish

exiles and supported not only their return to Jerusalem, but the rebuilding of the Temple. This was seen by the Persians as in their own interests – their reign would be longer and easier if the natives were kept friendly, but it gave Israel yet another chance. The Temple was rebuilt and the opening ceremony was marked by the reading of the five books of Moses by the prophet Ezra. What is so exciting about this part of the Bible is that so many non-Jewish historical records of the time back up the Bible's own account of this time. Despite the triumphal return, the five centuries that followed, up to the life of Christ, were characterised by one invasion after another. The Ancient Greek Empire, followed by the Roman one, until the Temple was finally destroyed by the latter in 66AD. This brings us back to the time our study began at – when the first gospels were being written and the early church, as recorded in the book of Acts, was bursting forth.

Read Daniel, chapter 6: putting God first.

Knowing God

I once heard a preacher describe how believers were often misleading in the way they described to other people the nature of the Christian life. He compared it to selling someone a cruise: we tell people to come to a dock where they expect to board a gleaming white ship. Instead they arrive and see a battleship. Expecting a name on the side, they see a number. There are no deckchairs to be seen, only gun turrets. They will find not a voyage of rest, but one of action and battles. The book of Daniel is the account of a man from youth to old age who preferred the battleship to the cruise ship.

Daniel knew that ultimately God is controlling history, that no matter how bad things may seem, his children will know Him through it. It is better to go through bad times with Him than good times without Him. We will struggle within ourselves and with those who'd oppose us, but the thing to remember is that in whatever situation, our God is ultimately in charge of history and we can know Him through His word, the Bible.

Printed in Great Britain
by Amazon